Legends of the Village

Legends of the **Village**

Photographers: Bela Borsodi, Craig Wallace Dale, Eve Fowler, Steve Hill
Research and Text: Andy Humm
Editor: Louis J. Ganim

VILLAGE CARE OF NEW YORK

Published by Village Care of New York
Book design: Designthing, Mark Von Ulrich, NYC

Printed in China
10 9 8 7 6 5 4 3 2 1

ISBN 978-0-9772416-3-7

Introduction

I once got in trouble for saying that the suburbs were sterile and boring. That really wasn't accurate. I should have said that the suburbs are a nice place to visit, but not for me on a permanent basis. I moved to the Village in 1956. In 1978, I moved into Gracie Mansion to serve 12 years as Mayor, and then returned in January 1990 to the Village where I plan to spend the balance of my life.

The Village celebrates diversity and non-conformity. In addition to being a great and tolerant neighborhood to live in, it is a place that people from all over the country and all over the world come to absorb some of its unique brand of freedom.

The Village has changed a lot over the years. It certainly is a much more expensive place in which to live. The Village with its activities fascinates the newcomers, and very quickly, the newcomer feels at home and becomes possessive, not wanting the ambience to change, and it doesn't.

For many, the Village is a charming, human-scale oasis in the midst of Gotham. The architecture and hodgepodge of streets make it unique in a Manhattan dominated by a relentless grid of streets and tall buildings.

In paging through this book of legends, you will see that the heart of the Village is mainly people—the individuals who have lived, worked and played here over the last century, bringing and developing their talents, creativity and determination to make not just the Village but the world a better place through the arts, politics, activism, religion, medicine, journalism and more.

I am privileged to be among such a wonderful group of people and hope that their stories—tales from true legends of the Village will inspire and entertain you as much as they did me. Some of those featured in this book are no longer with us, but their spirits—like the spirit of the Village itself—will always live on in people seeking to be free.

EDWARD I. KOCH

Foreword

Village Care of New York began the tradition of compiling the Legends of the Village calendar series in 1998 with the idea of creating a way to honor the famous and the unheralded who have contributed to the spirit of Greenwich Village. Each year, the calendars are used to help raise funds for the organization's wide range of care programs for seniors and for persons living with HIV/AIDS.

This volume compiles those individuals who were featured in the first ten editions of the calendar.

Like many of the legends featured in this book, Village Care got its start in Manhattan's Greenwich Village. In the mid-1970s, when a failed proprietary West Village nursing home threatened to leave much of Manhattan's West Side and downtown communities without a residential care facility for frail older adults, members of the community rallied together against great odds to acquire the home and create the not-for-profit Village Nursing Home.

Over the years, Village Nursing Home became a community icon, not because of the bricks and mortar of the historic building at Hudson and West 12th streets, but because the organization that grew out of that community movement has responded to evolving and emerging community needs. In the 1980s, this meant taking action in the face of the devastation of the AIDS epidemic as it swept across New York City, particularly Village neighborhoods. New, pioneering and innovative programs were created by Village Care to treat the disease and to address the many other needs of those living with HIV.

In the mid-1990s, it meant building upon the experience gained in the development of the organization's comprehensive Network of AIDS Services. Village Care addressed anew the needs of older adults with a vision of community-based care that seeks to delay, even prevent, institutional care with an array of programs called SeniorChoices that keeps individuals at home or in another community setting.

Village Care is dedicated to a mission of community care that is person-centered and where those who are served are partners in their care. By staying close to those in the community and recognizing what care and services they need, Village Care has been able to develop innovative responses in keeping with its vision and mission.

Village Care of New York, just as in its early days, is still about neighbors helping neighbors, which has long been a Greenwich Village tradition.

Bella Abzug

Bella Abzug became a community leader and an icon in the Village. "I was running for Mayor in 1977," she said, "when the Miami gay rights referendum was defeated by forces led by Anita Bryant. A huge late-night gay and lesbian demonstration formed in Sheridan Square to protest. They decided to march to my Bank Street home at 3 a.m. The funny thing was, my husband Martin and I were asleep when I was awakened by the sound of my name being called: 'Bella! Bella!' I woke up Martin and said that I heard my name being called out. He told me, 'You're dreaming, Bella! Go back to sleep!' I got out of bed, put on my dressing gown and went to the front door where there were thousands of demonstrators in the street. I told them we would fight this. I think that referendum was a turning point—the beginning of a backlash and fight back."

Bella Abzug grew up in the Bronx, her parents running the "Live and Let Live Butcher Shop." She became an attorney and fought for McCarthy's victims in the 1950s, founding the Women's Strike for Peace in the '60s. She was elected to the U.S. House of Representatives in 1970—one of 12 women there then—and championed civil rights and an end to the Vietnam War.

After narrowly losing the Democratic nominations for U.S. Senate in 1976 and mayor in 1977, she founded Women USA and the Women's Environment and Development Organization. She died in 1998 at the age of 77.

Edward Albee

PLAYWRIGHT, DIRECTOR, PRODUCER

"I remember the Village when it was a real village," Edward Albee said, who lives not far away now in his Tribeca loft. Greenwich Village played an enormous role in Albee's life and work. It was where he headed as a young man when he left his parents' suburban Larchmont home for good in the late 1940s. ("It had an awful reputation with people from Larchmont," he said.)

The Village was his home throughout most of the 1950s and into the '60s (with detours on the Upper East Side and Chelsea). Village playhouses were the venue for the first U.S. productions of such early plays as *The Zoo Story* (Provincetown Playhouse, 1960) and *Sandbox* (Cherry Lane, 1962) before the breakthrough Broadway success of *Who's Afraid of Virginia Woolf?*, starring Village legend Uta Hagen. (The title came from a graffito he saw in 1954 written with soap on the mirror behind the bar in the College of Complexes, then a West 10th Street bar/restaurant.

Albee's Village years—detailed with the rest of his life in Mel Gussow's excellent *Edward Albee: A Singular Journey*, 2001—included visits in the 1930s and '40s and living in several apartments, including one with budding playwright Terrance McNally, and a stint in the East Village. "It was a great time and place," he said, "for everyone starting out in the arts." As he honed his craft in the '50s, he worked such jobs as Western Union messenger and clerk in a record store.

When Albee became an international success with *Woolf*, "rather than just pay the government, I felt we should do something useful." Teaming up with Richard Barr and Clinton Wilder, he plowed much of his profit into producing young playwrights at The New Playwrights Unit Workshop, which "produced 110 new American plays," he said. Later, he established the William Flanagan Memorial Creative Persons Center, a writer's colony in Montauk. His reputation for generosity with his time and resources for young artists is as legendary as his playwriting.

Albee remembers great Village bars like the San Remo, Julius', and the Old Colony, that weren't "filled with Upper East Side attitude," he said. "Living in the Village and being a gay man, I never felt excluded or out of place. One was allowed to live one's life the way one wanted to."

Edward Albee has given us great theatrical works in six decades now. He won the Tony Award for *Woolf* in 1963 and was voted the Pulitzer Prize by their drama jury (only to have it outrageously withheld by the advisory board of journalists, one of whom called it "filthy"). He was awarded Pulitzers for *A Delicate Balance* (1967), *Seascape* (1975), and *Three Tall Women* (1993). In 1994, he received the Kennedy Center Honors from President Clinton in Washington. Among his numerous Obie Awards is one for Sustained Achievement. He has taught for decades at the University of Houston.

Jane Alexander

ACTOR, ARTS LEADER, HUMANITARIAN

Jane Alexander moved to New York in 1961. "I played the guitar and sang in coffee houses on Bleecker and MacDougal. I can remember I wasn't the weekend player—I was the one who played after the first set at 7 o'clock."

"I was a wannabe Joan Baez," she said, until she saw the real Joan Baez and was blown away. "She was so stunning." So Alexander stuck with acting and enjoyed a phenomenal career. "My very first paying job in New York was at the Sheridan Square Playhouse in 1961. It was Shaw's *Misalliance*. I played Lina Szczepanowska and Franny Sternhagen played Hypatia."

She briefly lived with her first husband at 213 W. 14th St. in a fifth floor walk-up. "I had this little baby and lived there five months before moving," she said. Her husband was a jazz aficionado and together they frequented Village clubs where she fondly remembers such acts as the jazz vocalists Lambert, Hendricks & Ross.

"Because I got involved with Broadway, the Upper West Side seemed easier to negotiate—especially with four boys. But I always loved the Village the most of any place in New York."

In 1976, she played Eleanor Roosevelt in *Eleanor and Franklin* on TV. "I did a lot of research on her and knew she had lived on Washington Square," she said. She was on stage at the Lucille Lortel playing novelist Djuna Barnes of Patchin Place in *What of the Night?*

Alexander won the Tony Award for playing Eleanor Backman in *The Great White Hope* on Broadway in 1969 and an Academy Award nomination for repeating the role on film. Six more Tony nominations followed as did three more Oscar nods. She was inducted into the Theatre Hall of Fame in 1994. But Alexander stepped into one of her greatest roles in 1993 when President Clinton picked her to head the National Endowment for the Arts, bringing stability to an agency wracked with controversy. Her acting continued, though, including a memorable turn as Sara Delano Roosevelt in HBO's "Warm Springs" in 2005.

Married to director and producer Ed Sherin since 1975, she is also dedicated to world peace, wildlife conservation and wellness—particularly for stroke patients.

Anthony Amato

DIRECTOR AND FOUNDER, AMATO OPERA COMPANY

With his dear late wife Sally—another Village legend—Anthony Amato has brought the joy and artistry of opera to the Village for more than half a century. They lived on Sheridan Square when they were married and their Amato Opera Company first performed in the hall of Our Lady of Pompeii on Carmine Street. "We had to get out for bingo games," he remembered. When the company opened a theatre on Bleecker Street, they performed for free and got by on donations, an average of 50 cents—"enough to cover costs."

Tony started as a singer for a number of opera companies, but was disappointed at the inattention to acting in productions of the day. "I gave up my singing career to run a 'drama in opera' workshop," he said.

In 1964, they needed a new theatre. They had been using 319 Bowery on the corner of Second Avenue, a pretty dicey neighborhood at the time, for storage and decided to convert the whole building into a 107-seat theatre. "I got it for a song," Tony said. "It is a place for young artists to sing before a live public in a professional atmosphere." Sally was a leading soprano with the company, in addition to being key to running the operation with Tony. It is the only self-sustaining opera house in the United States. In 2003, they did *La Traviata*, *Madame Butterfly*, *Andrea Chemier* and the *Barber of Seville* from the repertory of more than 60 operas at their command.

Some singers with the Amato Opera have gone on to the Met and the City Operas, but the company's motto remains, "Small, But Oh So Grand!"

Amy Ashworth

PARENTS AND FRIENDS OF LESBIANS AND GAYS PIONEER

Amy Ashworth was herself a nurse in Westchester when her son, Tucker, turned her on to contributing to saving the Village Nursing Home in the mid-1970s. But the real draw to the Village came in 1973 when she, her husband Dick and Tucker marched as a family in the Parents of Gays contingent of the Christopher Street Liberation Day March now known as the Lesbian and Gay Pride Parade.

"Four years later," she says, "our son Eric joined us and the four of us marched, Dick with his 'Proud Father of Gay Sons' sign and me with my 'We Love Our Gay Children' sign. We have always been overwhelmed by the response of the crowd, especially when we march into the Village. What is more natural than loving your children?"

Amy says that the parade has changed, as has her life. "We have the minute of silence at 2 o'clock for people who have died of AIDS. Tucker and Eric are among them. As we march into Sheridan Square, I always get a lump in my throat."

Dick and Amy moved to West 12th Street twelve years ago. "We've met the most wonderful people," she says. "We are there for them and they are there for us." In 1998, Dick died after 25 years as president of the Parents and Friends of Lesbians and Gays. Amy continues their work. She was born in Holland and lived much of her life here in the suburbs, but "the Village is my true home," she says.

Jean Bach

FILMMAKER

Jean Bach has lived in the Village since marrying Bob Bach in 1948. Their Charles Street digs had once been the original Nick's where jazz prevailed. The great acoustics there prompted one of their friends to borrow the space to record Dylan Thomas reading in a voice that the great Welsh poet described as "tenth-rate Laughton." But as he was pronouncing the words "and death shall have no do-min-ee-yun," a loud, shrill doorbell interrupted, prompting Thomas to let loose a string of epic vulgarities and ending that recording session.

The next Bach address was Washington Mews, a coach house turned into a dwelling in 1833. It was home at one time to artist and art patron Gertrude Vanderbilt Whitney ("Little Gloria had my bedroom," Jean says) and at another to music patron Alma Morgenthau. Jean immortalized the premises once more when she shot her Oscar-nominated film, "A Great Day in Harlem" there interviewing the jazz greats who had posed for that famous photo.

Kaye Ballard

ACTRESS

With 50 years in Greenwich Village, Kaye Ballard has more claim than most to her Village Legend status. "Palm Springs is wonderful," she said of her latest home while sitting in Washington Square Park fresh from doing a play on Long Island, "but this is where my heart is." She has had many Village apartments over the years—West 4th Street to 1 Sheridan Square, the latter was "one big room" and "downstairs was the old Café Society" that spawned Judy Holliday and Lena Horne, later housing the Theatre of the Ridiculous and Charles Ludlum.

"When I lived on West 4th Street in '47, I heard that John Barrymore had lived across the street and I would stare at that building," hoping some of the Barrymore magic would rub off. In those days, she hung out with Maureen Stapleton, Anne Jackson and Eli Wallach, dated Marlon Brando at the San Remo restaurant, and used to see Eleanor Roosevelt "in that building," pointing to the western side of the park.

Kaye Ballard has delighted audiences for decades in movies, radio, television, on records, and especially on stage. She started out in vaudeville, and toured with the Spike Jones Orchestra as a singer and musician. She did shows with Ray Bolger and Bert Lahr and *Touch and Go* in London where she was asked to do a Royal Command Performance at the Palladium.

She played nightclubs like the Village's Bon Soir in the 1950s, part of a long career in cabaret, and appeared regularly on almost every TV variety show you can think of—from *Perry Como* and *Ed Sullivan* to the *Tonight Show*. She and Eve Arden did the memorable sitcom *The Mothers-in-Law* in the late '60s.

Ballard introduced *Lazy Afternoon* in The Golden Apple on Broadway and made the cover of *Life* magazine, was in the original cast of *Carnival*, and played Ruth in *The Pirates of Penzance* for Joe Papp. She succeeded Ethel Merman as Mama Rose in *Gypsy* in the national tour. Her contributions in the documentary *The Golden Age of Broadway* are not to be missed.

You can read the whole Kaye Ballard story in her memoir, *How I Lost 10 Pounds in 53 Years* and by going to her website, KayeBallard.com.

Ann Bannon

NOVELIST

Ann Bannon, originally from the Midwest, was married and living in Philadelphia in the mid-1950s when the siren song of Greenwich Village sounded. She was drawn to the emerging lesbian subculture and spent weekends In New York exploring it. She also began translating her personal adventures into a series of pulp fiction novels, some about a character named Beebo Brinker. Critic Diane Hamer wrote that Bannon's books read "like a travelogue or tourist guide of Greenwich Village and its homosexual bars." Yet her novels are so much more, helping humanize lesbian life for readers in general and lesbians themselves.

"Coming back to the Village fifty years later the streets are right where I left them, though it was charmingly scruffy in the '50s and now everything is sleek and prosperous," she said at the Oscar Wilde Bookshop on West 4th Street on a visit back from California. Nevertheless, she remembers her time in the Village as one where she "never felt more free and full of possibility."

It was not all fun and games. "All of the gay bars got raided in those days on a schedule and patrons were tossed into police wagons," she said, noting that she was never present for a raid herself, but was always scared. "I could have lost my children," she said. Despite developing a nascent sense of community with others leading double lives, "we didn't have a glimmer that we were the first wave of a coming movement; nobody foresaw Stonewall," Bannon said, referring to the 1969 rebellion in the Village that sparked the gay revolution.

Today, Ann Bannon and her prescient, insightful works are celebrated by generations of readers after Stonewall.

Wayne Barrett

JOURNALIST, THE VILLAGE VOICE

One of the most tenacious political reporters in the history of the City of New York, Wayne Barrett had his first article in the *Village Voice* in 1972 and was given a regular column (called "Running Scared") in 1978. He is still doing his best to keep the powerful honest and the public informed through his *Voice* reporting and such books as *City for Sale* (with Jack Newfield) about municipal corruption, *Trump: The Deals and the Downfall*, and *Rudy! An Investigative Biography*, published in 2000.

Barrett grew up in Lynchburg, Virginia, and first came to New York to attend the Columbia School of Journalism in the heady year of 1968 when campus protests against the Vietnam War and Columbia's role in the community were an almost daily occurrence. He has lived in Brooklyn since then, first in Ocean Hill-Brownsville and now in Windsor Terrace with his wife, Fran.

The intense and often chaotic politics of Greenwich Village have been a frequent subject for Barrett over the years. He vividly recalls the night in 1989 when the Village Independent Democrats (VID), the home club of three-term Mayor Ed Koch, withheld its endorsement. "It's something that could only happen in the Village," Barrett said, "where there are enough people who would put principle over the substantial favors that an incumbent mayor can do for you, especially in his home base." He has also covered the battles between VID, a far left club, and its challenger, the Village Reform Democratic Club, which would be seen as almost as left by anyone outside the unique battleground of the Village.

The article Barrett is most proud of, however, is a cover story he did for the *Voice* in the early 1980s. "It was the first story written about IV drug use and AIDS when everybody thought it was just a gay disease. It took me to welfare hotels where people were in the late stages of dying from it, and I realized that I was in the middle of a dramatic change in human history. The story helped reshape the image of the plague."

Mordy and Irma Bauman

PERFORMING ARTISTS AND SOCIAL ACTIVISTS

Mordecai (Mordy) and Irma Commanday Bauman, who met singing together in the first Britten/Auden opera, *Paul Bunyan* in 1941, have lived in the Village part-time since the 1950s and permanently since 1978. Mordy was active in the musical life of the Village in the '30s in the Workers' Music League, the Theater of Action, singing and recording songs of Charles Ives, Elie Siegmeister, Marc Blitzstein, Hanns Eisler and others. The Baumans sublet an apartment on West 13th Street in the '50s to interview students for Indian Hill, their summer arts workshop in Stockbridge, Massachusetts. Among the luminaries who attended are Frank Rich (now at *The New York Times*), Arlo Guthrie (folk singer), Ruth Laredo (distinguished pianist), and Julie Taymor (director of *The Lion King*).

Mordy Bauman appeared in Sean O'Casey's *Within the Gates* with Lillian Gish, directed by Melvyn Douglas. He performed with the Phoenix Theater in Earl Robinson's and Waldo Salt's *Sandhog* about the men who dug the Brooklyn Battery Tunnel. In the Broadway Revue *Let Freedom Sing* he introduced the song *The House I Live In* by Lewis Allen and Earl Robinson.

A visit to Leipzig in 1978 to see the St. Thomas Church where Bach worked for 27 years, prompted Bauman to do something about Bach's 300th birthday in 1985. With a grant from the NEH, the Baumans produced the PBS program *The Stations of Bach*, broadcast nationally in 1990.

Mordy talked about how the Village has a leftover quality—an aura of what happened here in the early part of this century with writers like Eugene O'Neill and composers like Aaron Copland. "You knew you were a misfit in society, but in the Village everybody was."

The Indian Hill archives are in the Stockbridge Library; Bauman archive is in the Tamiment Collection at New York University.

Norma Becker

MOTHER OF THE PEACE MOVEMENT

Norma Becker moved to 68 Charles St. in the Village in 1966 in part to save her marriage to an artist, but ended up more successful in her singular quest to save the world. "I was a nonconformist rebel," she said. "I thought living in the Village would help us." The marriage didn't last, but the apartment became an informal headquarters for civil rights activists and the movement against the war in Vietnam. She also remembers that "when children ran away from home, they went to Diane and Gene's house," her kids.

While Becker taught public school in Harlem for 33 years, she will be most remembered as an extraordinary community organizer for peace and social justice here and around the world. She founded the Fifth Avenue Peace Parade Committee that turned out more than 25,000 for the first significant demonstration against the escalating Vietnam War and bringing together disparate factions to send one message.

Becker remembers the contentious meetings at 5 Beekman Street downtown, the headquarters of the pacifist movement. "We fought about everything from the color of the leaflets to the slogans," she said. "I was new and said, 'If people in this room can't get together on a slogan, I'll call others and march with one slogan.'" They did march behind the banner "End the Vietnam War Now." The numbers were "a shock to everyone but me," she said. It made front page news and even got a fashion story on what clothes the protesters wore.

She was a lead organizer of many of the protests in New York and Washington against the war after that and served as chair of the Village-based War Resisters League from 1977 to 1983. The Mobilization for Survival that she helped found organized the biggest anti-nuke demonstration in U.S. history in 1982 in Central Park.

Norma Lee Becker died on June 17, 2006, shortly after this interview at her apartment on Seventh Avenue and 14th Street. "One of the truly greats has passed," wrote peace activist David McReynolds, himself a Village legend, "one who might have changed the world if she had done nothing more than be a remarkable teacher, beloved by her students," but her work extended to the movements for peace and civil rights "at a time of profound risk."

"The Village isn't the community it used to be," Becker said, "but I still wouldn't want to live anywhere else." It is much diminished without her in it.

Rev. Daniel Berrigan, SJ

PRIEST, PEACE ACTIVIST, AUTHOR, POET

Rev. Daniel Berrigan, a Jesuit priest, is best known for his tireless witness for peace and justice, whether against the Vietnam and Iraq wars or seeking nuclear disarmament. He went to jail repeatedly for his protests and produced a body of more than 50 books of poetry, prose and drama, including *The Trial of the Catonsville Nine.*

But there is a less public Daniel Berrigan who has ministered to the poor and dying for decades, especially right here in New York. When the AIDS epidemic struck in the 1980s, he had been working with people dying of cancer at St. Rose's Hospice on the East Side. "We heard rumors of something terrible happening and learned of a pioneering program started by Sister Patrice Murphy in the Village," he said of AIDS ministry at St. Vincent's Hospital.

"I saw some pretty cruel things that had been going on in the hospital," said Berrigan, "meals being left at doors, chaplains giving blessings from the doorway and scuttling away. I refused to wear the white robes and masks like a KKK outfit. I envisioned patients waking up and seeing a hooded figure."

While he and his colleagues at first visited patients just when they came in for hospital care, Berrigan felt he wasn't getting to know any of them well enough to be of much help. He sought and was approved for an assignment to two or three people with AIDS, visiting them in their homes for as long as they lived. They often asked him to do their funerals. "I saw families that were devoted and came long distances," he said, "and others who were absolutely indifferent—whose ill and dying had no one but myself and the team."

In *We Die Before We Live,* his book about his experience at St. Rose's, he wrote, "I am beginning to sense it; you have to be in good form spiritually to work here." He also published a diary of his AIDS work, *Sorrow Built a Bridge: Friendship & AIDS* (1989).

Daniel Berrigan has a long acquaintance with death, whether the thousands of deaths he railed against in Vietnam or his own near death while in prison. Of his work in the 1980s with people with cancer and AIDS he says, "I was seeing more deeply what it is to be a human being and mortal and those people were helping me."

Karl Bissinger

PHOTOGRAPHER AND DRAFT COUNSELOR

Gore Vidal once wrote, "For more than half a century, whenever anyone asks me about the postwar 1940s and what it was like, I always say look at Karl Bissinger's photograph of us in the first issue of *Flair*," referring to a 1949 photo of Vidal with Tanaquil Le Clercq, Donald Windham, Buffie Johnson and Tennessee Williams at the Café Nicholson's garden patio in New York in 1949.

The Luminous Years: Portraits at Mid-Century by Karl Bissinger includes that photo and pictures of such icons as Jean Renoir, Colette, Truman Capote, Jean Cocteau, Gary Cooper, Marlon Brando and Tallulah Bankhead, among many others.

"When I first came to New York, I moved to the Village and went to the Art Students League," Bissinger said, sharing an apartment above the Cherry Lane Theatre, which, he reminds us, "was once on Cherry Lane when the Village was a village."

He was one of the early residents of Westbeth, the artist's complex on West Street, where he has lived for more than 40 years, many with his companion Dick Hanley who died in 1993. Living there, he says, "means I can afford to live in Manhattan. We have an art gallery, and several theatres and the Actors Studio is moving in. You're in contact with everyone from the art world."

In addition to his photography, Bissinger has a passion for social justice. "During the Vietnam War years, I went to the Quakers and took a course in draft counseling," he said, and then worked at the Greenwich Village Peace Center and later at the nearby War Resisters League for more than 20 years. After the Vietnam War ended, he led the WRL's fight for amnesty for draft evaders. He was recently presented with the group's Peace Award.

Bissinger's pacifism grew out of his experience growing up just after World War I. "It was such a terrible war," he once told interviewer Michael Moranna, "a war which should never have been fought. Nobody wanted to go to war again.

Patti Bown

SINGER, COMPOSER, SATIRIST, ACTRESS, AUTHOR

Patti Bown grew up in Seattle, but always dreamed of living in the Village. "I knew my soul was there," she said. A restless toddler, she didn't start to settle down until her mother brought a piano into the house when she was two. "It was the first time I could sit still and be amused for hours. There I felt peace," she said.

Bown did not make it to New York until the end of the 1950s. Though a childhood friend of Quincy Jones, she wasn't really accepted at first into the jazz world then because of prejudice against women. "Quincy would tell men, 'Let her sit down and play,' and they heard me and that was that." She traveled with his band all over the country and throughout Europe, but always liked returning to the "friendliness" of the Village. "I was born with a smile," Bown said.

In Greenwich Village, Patti Bown has played the Village Gate, Sweet Basil and Knickerbocker, among other venues. She has also played numerous concerts at Carnegie Hall, the Kennedy Center in DC and the JVC Jazz Festival. One of her many records is titled, *Patti Bown Plays Big Piano!* She has recorded everything from Duke Ellington to rap. Her life story was filmed by the Library of Congress. In 1976, she was brought out to Seattle by the mayor and governor to entertain Soviet officials to show them that we had more in common than we had differences.

Bown, a longtime resident of Westbeth, loves the buildings in the Village, saying, "I hope they never tear them down." But most of all she loves the people.

Jimmy Breslin

JOURNALIST

Ronnie Eldridge

POLITICAL LEADER

Although Jimmy Breslin and Ronnie Eldridge are an Upper West Side couple living where Eldridge was a crusading City Council member for many years, each has a special association with the Village. Breslin's Pulitzer Prize for Distinguished Commentary in 1986 was for a series of columns on AIDS, the first to "put human beings in the stories, not just medical statistics." Breslin had met David Camacho, a young Village political activist rapidly deteriorating from then-unstoppable HIV, at Uncle Charlie's Downtown on Greenwich Avenue (now an Irish pub called Fiddlesticks). "He was a lovely guy, an active fella," said Breslin. "All of a sudden you had sick people or people afraid of being sick. I knew them well. They're all gone now." He also remembered the old Village where "everybody wanted to write a novel." Breslin, who did write several in addition to countless trenchant newspaper columns, thinks now though that the Village has gotten "too classy."

Something that hasn't changed, Breslin says, is that the Village "was always known as a place to go at night."

Before there were community boards, Eldridge headed a task force in the Village for Mayor John Lindsay in the 1960s. She remembers organizing a tenants committee at an SRO hotel over the Village Gate—the Mills Hotel for Indigent Men, now the Atrium. In those days, however, it was, "a wild place," she said.

Eldridge also encountered early gay activists such as Marc Rubin who, she relates, "came to see me because police were telling them a parade permit was required for men to hold hands on the street," and Allen Roskoff who "chained himself to the mayor's desk." She helped, as she did with so many oppressed constituents for so many years. She was Lindsay's liaison to the first gay pride march in 1970, commemorating the Stonewall Riots on Christopher Street. And she ran Allard Lowenstein's campaign for Congress in the Village.

Breslin and Eldridge are still agitating for a more just society, Jimmy in his writing and Ronnie on "Eldridge & Co." on CUNY-TV.

Susan Brownmiller

FEMINIST WRITER AND ACTIVIST

Susan Brownmiller is the author of the feminist classics *Against Our Will: Men, Women and Rape* (1975) and *Femininity* (1985) and recently published *In Our Time: Memoir of a Revolution*, a history of radical feminism. And she is internationally renowned for her feminist critique of pornography.

Brownmiller grew up in Brooklyn, attended Cornell University, did civil rights work in Mississippi, and went to Philadelphia to be a TV reporter, but returned to New York without an apartment. She stayed with friends in the Village, but "at first I didn't want to live there," she said. "My parents thought it was Sodom and Gommorah. But it had the charm that I had found in Philadelphia—like sweet, low buildings." Now a longtime resident of Jane Street, "I'm one of those people who seldom goes above 14th Street unless I have to," she said.

"The real secret of New York that people out of town don't know," Brownmiller explained, "is that this is a city of neighborhoods." This particular neighborhood has undergone "remarkable" changes in her time. "When I first used to come down to the Village in the '50s, the beats were around and actors hung out at Louie's in Sheridan Square. I wanted to be an actress, then a TV news writer. When I moved here, I wrote for the *Voice*. I lived on Bleecker Street and would stay up all night and drop off my copy in Sheridan Square on Monday morning. I wrote about radical politics and race relations. I had the first story in the white press on James Brown. I wrote about Washington Square and Howard Moody at Judson Church. I settled into Village life and eventually my mother would come to visit and she was charmed by it."

Brownmiller said that the Village "has always been a good place for writers. When feminism started in the early 1960s, it was centered around the East and West Village. Florence Rush moved into my building. Nancy Stearns lives on Bank Street. Ann Koedt lived on Carmine Street. We belonged to a consciousness raising group called West Village One—the first West Village brigade of New York Radical feminists." She also mentioned Village writers such as Grace Paley, Alex Kates Schulman and Donald Barthelme. She studied acting with Joe Chaikin. Brownmiller's novel, *Waverly Place*, based on the Steinberg-Nussbaum child abuse case, is rooted in Greenwich Village.

"When I first moved here, Djuna Barnes walked along these streets," she said. "I hope that they say that about me."

Susan Brownmiller has a website at www.SusanBrownmiller.com

Ed Burnett

FATHER OF DIRECT MARKETING

Ed Burnett lived in the Village for almost forty years. He is best known as a pioneer in the field of direct marketing. His firm Burnett, Brenner became Database America and he retired from it in 1999.

Ed Burnett is modest about his role in saving the Village Nursing Home. His good friend, the late Lenore Zola, got him involved and he "only" served on the board for 21 years. He brought his acumen as the "father of direct marketing"—a title he acquired through his work at Database America—to saving the home. "The early years were tumultuous," he says of the nursing home board. "We didn't have much money. The records of the VNH were in cardboard boxes. It had almost been run like a toy by a private company that had to leave it."

Burnett used his "computer head" to put things in order, eventually developing a detailed list of donors to the home that topped 20,000. It took a whole Village to save the Village Nursing Home, but Lenore Zola and Ed Burnett and their friends did it. Ed passed away in 2005 at 90.

Charlotte Carter

WRITER

Mystery writer Charlotte Carter first came to New York from Chicago "at the height of the hippie era" and stayed for a summer in "a commune on Avenue D" decades before gentrification. She returned in 1972, settling in the East Village, getting into the downtown poetry scene. "The St. Mark's Poetry Project was pretty wild," she said, recalling Allen Ginsberg and his followers there. Soon she got interested in mystery fiction, the kind that would lead her eventual successes with *Rhode Island Red, Coq Au Vin, Drumsticks* and *Walking Bones.*

In the mid-1970s, though, she moved to "a tiny apartment" on Morton Street in the West Village, which she describes as "very Raymond Chandler pink Spanish-style 1930s Los Angeles." She lived "around the corner from James Baldwin," whom she would see in El Faro. Artist Maya Deren lived on her block. She remembered a wonderful old coffee house, now gone, called Maurizio, and the Cookie Bar near the White Horse Tavern.

For a time, Carter moved with a boyfriend to Village-like places in Montreal and then in Tangier for a writing workshop with Paul Bowles and finally in Paris "to escape Reaganomics in 1982." She then returned to New York

Nanette, her most famous literary creation is a Village denizen, "a jazz musician who mostly plays on the streets" and "loves life, food, music, drinking and men." Her new mystery series starts with *Jackson Park* back in Chicago in the 1960s, about a young woman who becomes a detective with two older relatives.

She is married to a crime writer, Frank King, about whom she said, "We had a working relationship that turned into a marriage."

Kathleen Chalfant

ACTRESS

Whether showing us how to die as professor Vivian Bearing in *Wit* or articulating the heart of the play in *Angels in America* as Prelapsarianov, "the world's oldest living Bolshevik"—among her multiple roles in Tony Kushner's opus—award-winning actress Kathleen Chalfant has been thrilling theatre audiences for decades, as well as through television and movies.

Her home base since 1995 has been in the West Village with her husband of 40 years, photographer and documentarian Henry Chalfant. They have lived in New York since 1973, moving downtown after rearing their children, David and Andromache, on the Upper West Side.

The Village house, while containing separate living spaces, was once shared with her brother, Alan Palmer, who died in 1998, and is still shared with her husband's cousin, artist Charles Ramsburg and his wife, author Michele Zackheim. "Everyone told us not to do it—live with family—but it seems to be working out OK," she said. "We didn't plan it. We fell into it. To make it work, you have to have your own door and your own kitchen—you have to have great respect for one another's privacy. It is a wonderful thing in time of trial and in happier times you have people to celebrate with."

Chalfant loves the Village. "When you look outside, it's beautiful and that's good for the human spirit," she said. "That is something that those of us privileged to experience it must appreciate and we must do all we can to make such beauty available to everyone."

Born in San Francisco and raised in the Bay Area, Chalfant said of acting, "I never wanted to do anything else." And so she came to New York at 28 "because that's where actresses come."

Chalfant has played Village stages many times, including the Public, Lucille Lortel, and Minetta Lane. She also lends her considerable talents to the boards of the Vineyard Theatre, Broadway Cares/Equity Fights AIDS and the New York Foundation for the Arts. She is a member of Madre, an international human rights organization, and is an adviser to Theaters Against War.

Ramsey Clark

ATTORNEY

When he left Washington in 1969 after serving as President Lyndon Johnson's Attorney General, Texas-born Ramsey Clark settled in Greenwich Village with his wife, Georgia, whom J. Edgar Hoover once dismissed as "nothing but a hippie" because she greeted him barefoot in her D.C. home.

Hoover, as discredited a public figure as there is in America, had even harsher words for Ramsey. The Clarks were hardly hippies, but Ramsey Clark has been described as having the "endearing demeanor of a country lawyer." His office on E. 12th Street is not far from where he resides.

Clark's leftist politics and advocacy for the oppressed have been remarkable even by Village standards. He went from opposing the Johnson administration's war in Vietnam to opposing most every act of aggression by the United States over the past three decades, particularly in Iraq. He made a couple of unsuccessful runs for the United States Senate seat from New York in the 1970s, but never gave up on the causes dear to him. His life has been about campaigning for peace, representing underdogs, fighting the death penalty and taking unpopular positions—as well as taking on unpopular "clients" ranging from international tyrants to Al Qaeda detainees at Guantanamo Bay naval base—in the pursuit of justice here and around the world.

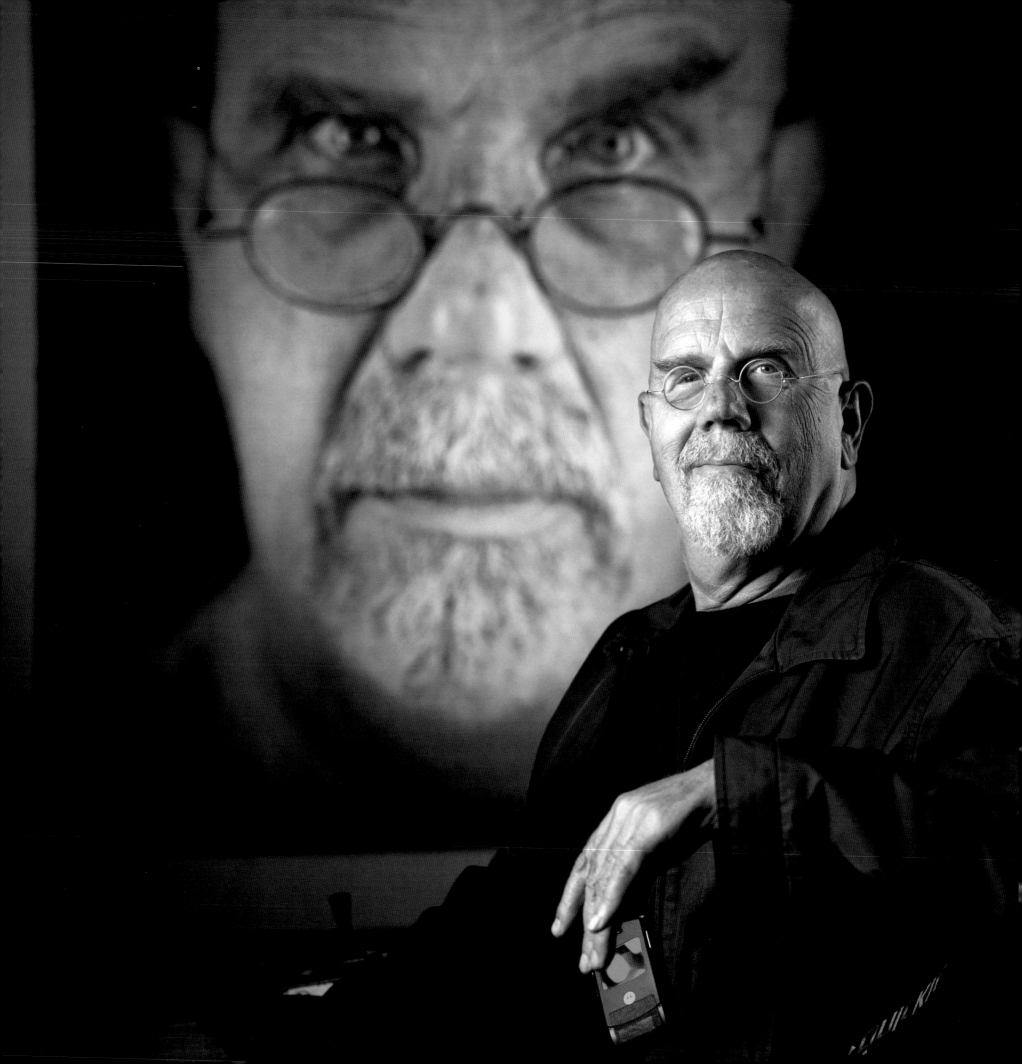

Chuck Close

ARTIST

When our photographer met Chuck Close in his Noho studio, the artist told Craig Wallace Dale, "I'm putty in your hands."

Dale said, "I was a little afraid to come here today because I rarely see a picture of you smiling."

"I'm not as grim as I look," Close said as he patiently moved through a range of poses and some smiles for Dale, just as he has patiently created some of the most iconic paintings of our time—massive portraits with intimate details that invite long and rewarding viewing.

Close grew up in a small town in Wisconsin and went to school in Seattle and New Haven—where he got his MFA at Yale—but considers himself "a downtown kind of guy." Though he lived in a variety of lofts and apartments in the Village and Soho after coming to the city in 1967, he and his wife raised their kids on the Upper West Side to be near their schools. "I never felt comfortable up there" where "a big building can have the population of Tribeca."

Close is happy to be living in the West Village now, "a small town in a big city." His Morton Square apartment "looks south and west and I can see down to City Hall and the Statue of Liberty and up the river."

He also has a view of the endless streams of traffic up and down the West Side Highway, which attract his artist's eye. "I love looking at the white jewels going one way and the red jewels the other," he said, giving beauty and richness to a landscape that most just see as a means to an end.

As the 2007 calendar was going to press, Close was fighting to preserve the light that has flooded his studio on Bond and Lafayette since 1985 from a developer who wants to put up a tower that would blot out the sun. "Nobody wanted this neighborhood," he told *The Villager*. "We [artists] saved it."

If Close cannot stop the overdevelopment, he will probably have to leave the City. "This can't be easily duplicated," he told the paper. "If I lose my light, I'm gone."

Close, who knew he wanted to be an artist from the age of four, once told *The New York Times*, "I wanted to make large, aggressive confrontational images that knock your socks off." Our major museums accord him some of their most prominent exhibition spaces. It would be a crime if our City was to drive him out from his own space, the scene of so many stirring works that give the neighborhood its worldwide reputation for creativity.

THE
BITTER
END

HANGING OUT AT AMERICA'S NIGHTCLUB

FOR SALE IN BOX OFFICE

Paul Colby

Paul Colby, who launched so many young talents as manager of The Bitter End at 147 Bleecker St. from 1968 on, got his start in show business in the 1940s working out of Tin Pan Alley with such greats as Benny Goodman, Frank Sinatra and Duke Ellington. In 1974, he became owner of the quintessential Village club and from then on it was "Paul Colby's Bitter End."

Coming from the uptown music scene, "people in the Village were foreign to me," he said. "I was a Cole Porter fan." But he got to know the Village crowd and whom they liked. John Sebastian, Kris Kristofferson and Judy Collins are among his friends from those days. He gave Billy Crystal a break, putting him under contract for $50 a show. For Neil Young and James Taylor, it was their first time on a stage. For Bill Withers, it was his first appearance anywhere. Andy Gibb was appearing just as his first album hit the top of the charts.

"I had the pleasure of introducing people and saying, 'This one is going to be a star!'" That's still something Paul Colby can say in a Village institution that endures to this day—one of the first places Czech President Vaclav Havel visited when he came to the United States.

In his autobiography, *The Bitter End: Hanging Out at America's Nightclub* (Cooper Square Press, 2002), Colby writes, "The music and comedy of [the '60s] informed our politics, social behavior, morals and love life. Never before had music played such an integral part in the politics and manners of our country. Not since Jonathan Swift had humor been so stinging, scathing and devastatingly honest."

Judy Collins

SINGER, SONGWRITER, HUMANITARIAN

Judy Collins grew up in Seattle where her talent was nurtured at ten by Dr. Antonia Brica, the orchestral conductor, about whom she later made an Academy Award-nominated film. Collins is a world-renowned artist, but the intimacy of her singing originated in the little clubs she played first in Denver and then in Greenwich Village as the 1960s dawned. It was in 1961 after an appearance at the Village Gate that she was offered her first recording contract by Electra where she stayed for 24 years.

Collins once lived in the Village at 135 West 10th St. on the tenth floor, overlooking the Hudson. She worked Gerde's Folk City, "where we saw the most amazing things," including Bill Cosby originating his legendary "God and Noah" sketch. Over at the Bitter End she remembers Joan Baez, Tom Paxton and Tom Chapin among many others.

A Westsider now, she said, "If I had found a big apartment in the Village, I would still be down there. It's still such a great place to come. One thing a lot of us learned down there was how to pay the rent."

Today, Collins is still singing, now on her own label, Wildflowers, and working for such causes as UNICEF. She has given us music for our souls from *Both Sides Now* to *Send in the Clowns* to *Song of Sarajevo*, combining her passions for art and social justice.

The plaque reads:

ELEANOR ROOSEVELT

RESIDED AT
20 EAST 11TH STREET
FROM 1933 TO 1942

Blanche Wiesen Cook

HISTORIAN, WRITER, LESBIAN FEMINIST PIONEER

Blanche Wiesen Cook is now famous for her award-winning, multi-volume biography of Eleanor Roosevelt who lived in the Village. But Cook, a lesbian feminist pioneer, has her own fond memories of the place in the 1950s. In an article, "The Radical Women of Greenwich Village" (from the book, *Greenwich Village: Culture and Counterculture*) she writes: "We could hold hands in the Village and think reckless thoughts, and read banned books and forbidden magazines, and look ardently into each other's eyes. We were sure we were not alone, but we really did think we were the first. And for so many years there were no books, no articles, no poems to tell us differently."

Historian Cook wrote of how the Village "became the headquarters from which Roosevelt began to pursue her long career as an independent political activist after 1920" when she learned of FDR's affair with Lucy Mercer. Eleanor frequently spent evenings at the 20 East 11th St. home of Esther Lape and Elizabeth Read, "her political mentors and best friends." In the 1930s, during FDR's presidency, Eleanor rented an apartment in the Lape-Read home as "a haven for herself and her own company, a secret place hidden away from the glare of newspapers and photographers." Cook continued: "Toward the end of FDR's third term, she began to consider life after first ladyhood and decided to move into a larger space at 29 Washington Square West, where on occasion her husband might join her—but only on occasion"

Eleanor Roosevelt chose the Village, "for its attractive environment and its free-thinking anonymity—as seems only appropriate given the hectic nature of her free-thinking, heterodox life."

Betty Comden and Adolph Green

SONG-WRITING TEAM AND PERFORMERS

Betty Comden and Adolph Green remembered how stars were born. Betty said, "On a rainy night in 1938, 17-year-old Judy Holliday came down the stairs of Max Gordon's old Village Vanguard. She met Max and they started talking about how he wanted to change the Vanguard. At the time, he only featured poets and was looking for a way to bring in a younger audience. Judy knew Adolph, Adolph knew me, and when he next ran into me at an audition, he told me about his conversation with Judy. Together, the three of us wrote our own show as the *Revuers*. That was the beginning of a collaboration with Adolph that has gone on for the last 58 years."

Together they wrote such memorable shows as *On the Town*, *Wonderful Town*, *The Band Wagon*, the musical of *Peter Pan*, *Applause* and the classic movie *Singin' in the Rain*. Included among the standards they wrote are *Just In Time*, *The Party's Over*, *Make Someone Happy*, *Neverland*, *Some Other Time* and *New York, New York*.

They won a shelf full of Tony Awards and the heartfelt love of the Broadway community.

Adolph Green died at age 87 on October 23, 2002, and Betty Comden at 89 on November 23, 2006.

Keith Crandell

VILLAGE COMMUNITY ACTIVIST

Keith Crandell, who moved here in 1971 when "a rapacious landlord drove us out of Chelsea," was the quintessential Village activist, a leader on Community Board 2 and with the Village Independent Democrats for all of those years. In this neighborhood with an increasing reputation for affluence, he always spoke up for the poor, the homeless, the mentally ill and people with AIDS.

"When I travel around the country and tell people I'm from New York City, they make a face," he says. "But when I tell them I live in Greenwich Village, they say that's nice. They have a specific relationship with Greenwich Village that they don't have with the rest of the city—a romance," he said.

He was often seen riding his "trademark, ten-speed clunker" bicycle all over the Village. Calling it "a damn good way of keeping in touch with what's going on and a great way of getting around. I'm on the traffic committee and know where all the potholes and traffic tie-ups are."

Mr. Crandell's fights for the Village environment have preserved much of what we all love about it—"the Village quality of it." He loved the shopping from the greenmarket in Union Square to the pasta at Raffeto's on Houston Street. "I just got back from Montana and Texas," he said for this interview, "and you don't see any places like this."

Keith Crandell died on May 28, 2005, at the age of 77.

Merce Cunningham

CHOREOGRAPHER AND MODERN DANCER

Merce Cunningham told us in 2000, "For the past 18 years, my studio has been in Westbeth, the old Bell Telephone Laboratories turned into housing for artists at the corner of Bethune and West Streets. It is there that our classes, rehearsals, and, at times, performances, have been held. It brought us back to the Village and to the atmosphere of a neighborhood where people sometimes even saunter in the streets and say 'Hello' to each other. The ambience of Westbeth, this large structure housing artists from the visual and performance arts who are able to work and live in the same space, is distinctly different from a business situation. The Village has changed certainly from when I came as twenty-year-old. But that sense of neighborhood that it had still clings."

Tony Dapolito

MAYOR OF GREENWICH VILLAGE

If you want to understand why the Village is preserved the way it is, you need to know about Tony Dapolito.

"I was born in 1920," he said, "the year my father opened the Vesuvio Bakery in the South Village that has always been my home. In 1950, when the one and only Robert Moses was planning to build a housing project that would have destroyed the neighborhood, I got active in the fight to stop it. We often fought Commissioner Moses and I think we were the only community to fight him successfully. His projects would have changed the Village forever. He wanted to build the Lower Manhattan Expressway and a depressed roadway right through Washington Square Park. By organizing local people into a powerful force supported by neighbors, we beat him. I think that we can credit Robert Moses with making more community leaders than anyone in New York City."

Tony Dapolito died on November 10, 2003, just a day shy of his 83rd birthday.

Samuel Delany

AUTHOR

Samuel R. Delany is one of our foremost science fiction writers, having won numerous Hugo and Nebula awards for his novels and stories. He was born in Harlem, and his 1988 autobiography, *The Motion of Light in Water*, deals with both the East and West Village. His latest novel, *Dark Reflections*, chronicles life around Tompkins Square. As well as writing his novels and memoirs, Delany has taught comparative literature, English, and creative writing at a number of universities, and he is now an English professor at Temple. Here are his reminiscences and reflections on the Village:

"In 1954 or '55, lugging my Martin-double-O/18 guitar in its hard case beside my knee, from Harlem where I lived and the Bronx High School of Science where I went to school, I hit the Village on a Sunday afternoon, to play with the myriad folksingers in Washington Square, who came in from all over the city, the country, to make music. I was thirteen. A bunch of singing groups followed, their names written only on time's sloshier currents, The Harbor Singers, Waldo and Oversoul (I was 'Oversoul'), even one called The East River Fuck Ups, and Heavenly Breakfast. I wrote songs and arranged music for them all and dreamed of record contracts and was happy. By now, with my then-wife, poet Marilyn Hacker, I'd moved to the East Village (and moved José Feliciano off our couch and into an apartment upstairs). But nights brought us west, to perform in Gerdes Folk City, the Gaslight, the Bitter End, and the Fat Black Pussy Cat—places all made famous by people other than us.

"And somewhere in there, I began to write—or, rather, to write more. It's a little unbelievable, even to me, that, by my mid-twenties, with half a dozen novels published (and living in the more affordable East Village, a fifteen-minute lope from MacDougal Street), when I did the math I was still making more from passing the basket in Liz's Place, between the rounds of go tiles clicking on the playing boards, or the Café Elysee (across from the famous Night Owl, where 'Zal, Denny, and Sebastian sat') than I was from writing—venues that never became famous, probably because I and my friends were singing there: and not Fred Neil, Richie Havens, Bob Dylan, Peter Tork and Tim Hardin, people who said hello to us, and sometimes even dropped by the apartment, but probably weren't sure of our names for more than a week or two at a time.

"It's an easy period to grow nostalgic for, when 'Who's Afraid of Virginia Woolf' was a graffito scrawled across the inside of the Ladies' Room door at the Café Figaro—as Marilyn reported to me, years before Edward Albee wrote his play—and there was a raw bar on MacDougal Street, just down from Bleecker, where littlenecks were a dollar a dozen.

"The spirit of New York City is there, somewhere, in all my novels. "

Neil Derrick

NOVELIST

Edward Field

POET AND NOVELIST

Neil Derrick, author of a series of paperbacks, one about the now-demolished women's prison on Greenwich Avenue, and his friend Edward Field, a much published, award-winning poet, got the idea for *The Villagers*, their historical saga covering 145 years of Greenwich Village history, from observing how the Village has changed in the decades they've lived here. A complaint of the characters throughout the novel is: "The Village is not what it was."

Brooklyn-born Field first came to Greenwich Village after World War II to attend New York University on Washington Square on the GI Bill, while Derrick, a Californian, arrived a decade later as a veteran of the Korean War to write fiction. They now live in Westbeth, the artists' housing development in the West Village, where Bell Labs, as part of the Manhattan Project, had designed the Norden Bombsight for the Flying Fortresses that Field flew in during the war. Field and Derrick started collaborating on fiction after Derrick lost most of his sight, and *The Villagers* is their latest project.

André De Shields

André De Shields is most famous for his roles on Broadway in *The Wiz, Ain't Misbehavin'* (for which he won an Emmy when it was on NBC in 1982), *Play On!* (for which he received his first Tony nomination), and *The Full Monty*, but he wanted his picture taken at the East Village's La MaMa Experimental Theatre Club where he worked with the legendary Ellen Stewart.

Born in Baltimore and educated at the University of Wisconsin at Madison, he first came to New York as a "struggling actor" from Chicago to play Desi Arnaz on Broadway in a science-fiction/adventure called *Warp*— "years before the *Star Wars* phenomenon," he noted. When the show only lasted 12 performances, "I had to make a life-changing decision," he said. "Do I stay here and cast my fate to fortune? It was the last time I slept in a park—Central Park, in fact—but I never felt poor, just broke."

"Kenny Rubenstein of La MaMa had seen me and told me, 'You've got the stuff,'" De Shields said. "I didn't know La MaMa, but was cast in *Sacred Guard* for $25 a week."

Ellen Stewart told him during that production, "Baby, Mama's gonna take care of you." He said that Stewart "taught me that an agent is the last thing you need. She told him, "you need an artistic home, you need to know about failure, and you need the opportunity to succeed again."

De Shields has done some work at La MaMa every year ever since—directing, acting, lecturing—"but it hardly pays back my debt," he said. He has added enormously to the luster of the theater through his acting, singing, dancing, choreography and directing, but his contributions go even deeper than that. He is past chair of Equity's Committee for Racial Equality. He has worked tirelessly for the restoration and enhancement of arts education in the public schools in the five boroughs and helping young people understand and relate to the legacies of such giants as Bessie Smith, Fats Waller and Louis Armstrong. He conceived two shows on Armstrong, *In Search of Pops* and another called *West End Blues: Louis Armstrong*.

André De Shields is brilliant whether stopping the show as the working-class Noah "Horse" T. Simmons in *The Full Monty* or teaching Shakespeare as an adjunct professor at NYU's Gallatin School of Individualized Study in the Village. He also received his M.A. in African-American studies from NYU.

Germán Diez

PIANIST AND TEACHER

Walk along leafy Barrow Street and stop outside the Greenwich House Music School, where Germán Diez has taught since 1959, during the day and you are almost sure to hear piano from the hands of one of his students.

Born in La Habana, Cuba, Diez won a national music award competition in 1945 there that allowed him to study abroad. Maestro Claudio Arrau granted Diez a personal scholarship to study with him in the United States for ten years during which time he played concerts here, in Cuba and in the West Indies, also appearing regularly on radio and television.

He has had brilliant students who have had great classical careers such as pianists Antoine Zemor, Bennett Lerner and Erika Nickrenz, as well as composer Joan Tower. But he also tells the story of two brothers, 8 and 11, who showed no promise at all for the piano. "I tried to get their mother to get them to take up another instrument. At their next lesson, they showed up dressed elegantly. When I asked why, they said, 'We are celebrating. This is our last lesson!'"

Far from giving his last lesson, Diez' work continues (he's chaired the Piano Department since 1968). And he expresses his love for the Village's unique character and reputation, which he knew of when he was growing up in far away Cuba. "It resembles Paris—the European atmosphere. It represents art in general."

Greenwich House Music School has established a piano scholarship in his name.

Art D'Lugoff

Art D'Lugoff, a legend among Greenwich Village legends, was also the maker of many a legend during his 36 years as impresario of the Village Gate, from 1958 to 1994. Aretha Franklin made her first New York appearance at his famous club at Bleecker and Thompson. Even before that, he rented out the Circle in the Square at midnight for Pete Seeger and Sonny Terry, along with then-unknown Mary Travers, 16, who would go on to fame with partners Peter and Paul.

"The Village was a place you could start out and do things," he said. "The prices were right on every level—business and living." Today he laments how quickly a business has to prosper in order to stay open.

Who played the Gate? Who didn't!

Journalist Jack Newfield remembers one show where D'Lugoff had singer Nina Simone, harmonica virtuoso Larry Adler and comedian Dick Gregory. "And he charged only four dollars," Newfield said.

D'Lugoff had jazz greats from Miles Davis to Wynton Marsalis. He did a "Salsa Meets Jazz" series that got everybody downtown. Comics from Woody Allen to Bill Cosby headlined there. The Gate was also a venue for topical theater like *Macbird* and hits like *Jacques Brel is Well and Alive and is Living in Paris*. Before there was a Saturday Night Live on NBC there was Chevy Chase and John Belushi in D'Lugoff's presentation of *National Lampoon's Lemmings*. D'Lugoff used the space too as a stage for intense political debates on the most contentious issues in a tumultuous time. Even D'Lugoff's staff was noteworthy: Dustin Hoffman waited tables, Sam Shepard washed dishes.

D'Lugoff today is an adjunct professor at NYU, and is helping initiate the National Folk Music Museum in the Village and a National Jazz Museum in Harlem.

E.L. Doctorow

AUTHOR AND TEACHER

E.L. Doctorow's great novels have often been set in New York, from *Ragtime* and *Billy Bathgate* to *World's Fair* and *City of God* with its special focus on the East Village. He is a distinguished professor at New York University.

The "E" in his name stands for Edgar, in honor of Edgar Allan Poe. While Poe is far from his favorite writer, Doctorow became deeply involved a few years ago in saving Poe's Village house on Amity (now W. 3rd) Street when NYU's Law School wanted to tear it down to make way for a new building.

"The Poe house," Doctorow wrote, "is one of the few still remaining of a literary cultural parcel that exists more in time than in space: Herman Melville roamed these precincts. Henry James was born just east of Washington Square. John Dos Passos, Edna St. Vincent Millay, Thomas Wolfe and e.e. cummings all lived at one time or another near the university. Mark Twain had rooms for a while on 10th Street just west of Fifth Avenue, and Walt Whitman's favorite saloon was Pfaff's on Broadway, a few steps north of Bleecker Street. The Poe house is quite small and very suggestive of the writer's perpetually straitened circumstances."

Largely due to the persuasion of Doctorow and other faculty, the school agreed to embed in the façade of the new Law School building a facsimile of the original Poe House façade, and some interior elements including a remnant of the elegant staircase.

E.L. Doctorow has won numerous literary prizes, including the National Book Award, two National Book Critics Circle Awards, the PEN/Faulkner Award, the Edith Wharton Citation for Fiction, the William Dean Howell Medal of the American Academy of Arts and Letters and the National Humanities Medal conferred by the President of the United States.

Dennis Duggan

REPORTER AND COLUMNIST

Pulitzer Prize-winning journalist Dennis Duggan lived in the Village for 35 years on various streets, most recently in a building owned by Frank Wolff whom he called "the city's best landlord." Duggan called his place "a house of music where everyone but me plays a musical instrument and where my porch looks out over the leafy backyards—just like *Rear Window*."

Duggan began his newspaper career at the *Daily Mirror*, joined the *Herald Tribune* in 1959, went to *The Times* in 1960, and then *back* to the *Tribune*, "because I loved the place—Breslin, Wolfe, Reeves, Portis and so on."

Lured to *Newsday* in 1968 when Bill Moyers offered him a job "in a new New York bureau of the paper out of which came *New York Newsday* that died in '95. We are now a shadow in the city."

In addition to his Pulitzer, Duggan was awarded the prestigious Meyer Berger Award from Columbia University and the Peter Kihss Award from the Society of Silurians. Mostly, he is famous for giving voice to hundreds of everyday New Yorkers, including many in his home base of the Village.

"I've been writing a three-a-week column for 20 years," he said for this interview, "covering City Hall, courts, and people. I've been all over the world, but New York City is number one by a mile."

Dennis Duggan died at age 78 on April 20, 2006.

Jules Feiffer

CARTOONIST, AUTHOR, PLAYWRIGHT

Jules Feiffer, Pulitzer Prize-winning editorial cartoonist, writes: "In October of 1956, I had been out of the Army for three years and had no luck in selling my work to anybody and only got in print in cartoons. When I did, it was junk for the marketplace—not at all representative of what I really did. In desperation I took myself to the offices of the *Village Voice*, at that time on Greenwich Avenue across from the Women's House of Detention.

"I walked upstairs to this small cluttered office and showed my work to all those present including Dan Wolfe, the editor, Ed Fancher, the publisher, Jerry Talmer, the culture maven, and John Wilcock, the gossip columnist. To my amazement—because up until then I had gotten nothing from people who counted—those who counted at the *Voice* liked my work and agreed to put me in the paper immediately doing anything I chose, the only drawback being they could not afford to pay me anything.

"I considered this the best offer I'd had in years and seized it. And my first strip, *sick, sick, sick*, appeared in the *Voice* a couple of weeks later and went on for the next 42 years under the name *Feiffer*."

How long was it before he started getting paid? "Eight years," he said. But being in the *Voice* "got the attention of all the publishers that were turning me down." His first collection was *sick, sick, sick*. His nineteenth book is for children: *The Daddy Mountain* from Hyperion. Feiffer says it is "about how my five-year old grandchild climbs her father, told in the first person."

He also speaks ironically about his "pro bono" work in the theatre, turning out such enduring works as *Little Murders*, *Knock Knock*, *Grownups* and *A Bad Friend* as well as such screenplays as *Carnal Knowledge* and the Oscar-winning short film, *Munro*. "After *Little Murders* flopped on Broadway," he said, "it was revived at the Circle in the Square on Bleecker Street under Alan Arkin's direction and ran for two years, salvaging my career as a playwright."

Crystal Field

DIRECTOR, THEATER FOR THE NEW CITY

The Theater for the New City was born in Westbeth in the West Village in 1971 and ended up on First Avenue at 10th Street where it thrives today. Crystal Field, its executive director, meanwhile has been a constant there for more than 40 years.

Field started out in Philadelphia in the 1960s writing and performing street theater against the Vietnam War. Her mission in New York—her New City—has been to nurture new writers rather than produce revivals of classics. When their space was threatened in the 1980s, they put together a rally of 4,000 people including Village performers like Spalding Gray, impresario Joe Papp, and political leaders such as City Council Members Miriam Friedlander and Ruth Messinger. They won.

"I love to act," Field said, "but I had to give it up to run this place. I was happy to." She is particularly proud of the outlet that her theater has provided for emerging writers who are African-American, Latino, gay and lesbian, women, Native American, and much more of the diversity that makes up New York. "We just want to do good theater," she said.

The plays you see at the Theater for the New City are not household names. "We only do new work," Field said. "Someone has got to develop and nurture new writers. They will be recognized as great writers ten years from now. We've become a port in a storm. And that's why we need the four theaters here."

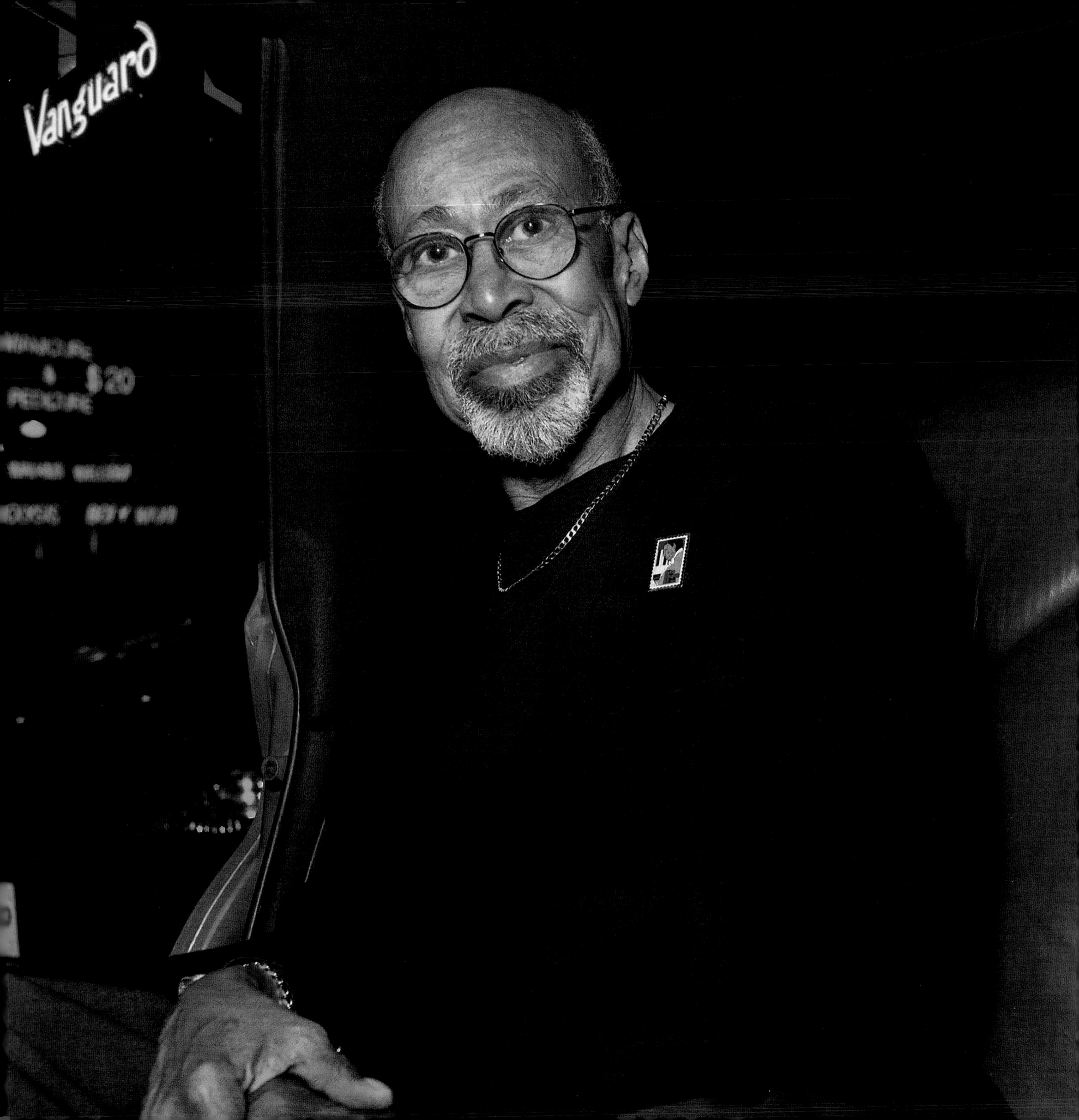
Vanguard

Tommy Flanagan

JAZZ GREAT

Jazz great Tommy Flanagan played in the Village for nearly half a century, starting in 1956.

"One of my first jobs," he said, "was in the Village Vanguard with a quintet made up of J.J. Johnson, Elvin Jones, Wilbur Little and Bobby Jaspar."

In those days, some of the beat poets shared the bill with the musicians, including Jack Kerouac reading from *On the Road*.

Flanagan remembered "people like Kenneth Tynan and Allen Ginsberg as the opening act for Thelonius Monk and Charles Mingus at the old Five Spot on 3rd Street and the Bowery. A couple of painters—like Larry Rivers—used to be in the house all the time, too." Flanagan said that the "atmosphere was much more hip than the rest of the city—much more open, just as it is today—very responsive to all kinds of groups."

Tommy Flanagan died on November 16, 2001. He was 71.

Miriam Friedlander

CITY COUNCIL MEMBER AND SOCIAL ACTIVIST

Miriam Friedlander of East 6th Street is one of the most passionate advocates of the downtrodden and disenfranchised in the city's history. First elected to City Council in 1973 at age 59, she served until 1991. When we spoke to her in 2001 at 86, she was still in the thick of things, organizing an annual conference on Women Fighting Poverty.

"I enjoy being one of the wonderfully varied 'People of the Village—East and West,'" she says. Her political work "was and still is constantly stimulated, enriched, and made more effective" by these people who respond to "any threats to our creative Village lifestyles, human and civil rights, historic housing, waterfront, clean water and air."

She is proud of the way Villagers were able to overcome fears and make way for special needs housing for people with AIDS, the disabled, youth and the homeless. "Most of them became positive and working neighbors."

She was one of the leaders in the battle for the city's gay rights law that finally passed in 1986 after a 15-year struggle, sticking up for her gay and lesbian neighbors when they were defamed at the public hearings.

When time came that her seniority accorded a committee chair on City Council, political leadership balked. But the Manhattan delegation in turn demanded she get her chair, and she did. Asked to suggest a theme, she explains: "I proposed and was given—after many 'whys?'—a Subcommittee on Women and soon we were going full blast on hearings on every facet of violations and inequities against women, effecting many changes in city policies and protections."

Barbara Garson

PLAYWRIGHT, JOURNALIST, ACTIVIST

Back in 1967 during the Vietnam War, Barbara Garson hit a cultural nerve with her anti-war play *MacBird*, a stinging satire aimed at both Presidents Johnson and Kennedy, first performed at the Village Gate. It ended up being performed all over the world and sold half a million copies. From her commitment to social justice and peace, she left her *MacBird* success to work in an anti-war coffeehouse for GIs near Fort Lewis. She had also edited the Free Speech Movement Newsletter at Berkeley in 1964. Her book, *Money Makes the World Go Around: One Investor Tracks her Cash Through the Global Economy*, is "part mystery and part anti-globalist manifesto" (Howard Zinn wrote, "This book shows her at her best, able to be funny about serious things and crystal-clear about impossibly complex matters.")

Sitting in her Westbeth apartment with a Ralph Lee-designed street scene set along one wall, she talks about her 1976 Obie-award winning children's play, *The Dinosaur Door*, for which she has been getting requests over the Internet because Vin Diesel acted in it as a child. "He lived in this building as a kid," she says, also noting that a young Tim Robbins had been cast in the original production but had to bow out because "his parents took him to Hollywood." She recalls, "Boy was he good!"

Garson worries about the Village. "Once they get rid of rent control there won't be any more Village legends," she said. "Listen to me saying 'it's the end of the Village.' In every period people who came here asked, 'What happened to the real Village?' But was it ever 'the Village,' or was it just our youth?" Always questioning. Always challenging. Never finished.

Joyce Gold

WALKING TOUR GUIDE AND HISTORIAN

Joyce Gold knows where the bodies are buried in New York—literally. And in some cases, she knows where their restless spirits still roam.

She is one of New York's premier historians, teaching courses on the history of the city at The New School and New York University. But she is perhaps best known as the leading walking tour guide in New York, taking groups through more than 20 city neighborhoods. Her most popular tour is called Macabre Greenwich Village.

Just north of the Village in her book-lined loft that she shares with her spouse, Leslie McKenzie, Gold said, "My job is make tourists out of New Yorkers as well as the reverse."

"There may be 10,000 people buried under Washington Square Park, mostly poor people," she said. "It was a potter's field." She can show you where the hanging structure once stood in that park. And she has a picture she took at Shearith-Israel Cemetery near Chatham Square in the 1970s of the tombstone of Richa Levy, who died around the time of the Revolution, that contains a blur that "had a very definite shape" and "looks like a ghost."

She said that there is one word for New York and that is "choice." "The epitome of that is Greenwich Village. You can do what you want and don't have to do what you don't want." She said the Village's bohemian character can be traced back to Pfaff's under Broadway at Bleecker, a hangout for Walt Whitman in 1859.

"New Yorkers don't know what they pass walking its streets every day," she said. "Everything is there for a reason and it tells about life a long time ago. There was a stream in the Village and that's why the law library at NYU gets a little damp on rainy days and why the pool there doesn't go deep."

The Village, she said, "is not only a place, but a state of mind—accepting a variety of people and ideas and holding on to what's valued."

For information on Gold's tours and books, go to www.nyctours.com

Frances Goldin

The Village would be nothing like the neighborhood we know and love were it not for the leadership of activists like Frances Goldin. Back in the 1950s, they stopped Robert Moses from building the Lower Manhattan Expressway that would have eliminated 10,000 apartments in Little Italy and the West Village. "The harm to the people would have been devastating," she said.

"When the Cooper Square Committee stopped it—this little organization—we realized that we could do anything."

Goldin moved to the Lower East Side from Queens when she married and has been an organizer for fair housing and human rights ever since. Growing up, she felt "isolated and hated." Living in what is now called the East Village ("a real estate term," she calls it), Goldin remarks, "I could not believe how deeply I could breathe.   It gave my children the best possible introduction to a multiracial world." Folks weren't able to stop the gentrification of her neighborhood but "we were able to slow it down."

For more than 30 years, she has run the Frances Goldin Literary Agency, representing such writers as Dorothy Allison, Barbara Kingsolver, Adrienne Rich, Susan Brownmiller, Ramsey Clark, Frances Fox Piven, Juan Gonzalez, Martin Duberman and Mumia Abu-Jamal, author of *Live from Death Row*. She works daily on the campaign to free Mumia from a Pennsylvania prison and has been arrested at the Liberty Bell in that cause.

"If you think you're going to do something overnight," this veteran organizer said, "forget it, it takes years." But Frances Goldin has brought the kind passion and creativity to her causes that have kept her work alive and effective for more than 50 years.

Lesley Gore

SINGER AND SONGWRITER

While many singers got their start in the Village, Lesley Gore played clubs like Reno Sweeney's there long after she was an internationally famous star. She performed there in the 1970s when "wondrous artists like Peter Allen and Melissa Manchester and the Manhattan Transfer" were playing, she said. "There was no dressing room, though. We used a coat closet."

Back in the 1960s, Gore had been discovered by Quincy Jones when singing at a Manhattan hotel. He produced her #1 hit, *It's My Party*, and she became a teen sensation, scoring more hits with *Judy's Turn to Cry*, *She's a Fool* and *You Don't Own Me*, and performing on the big screen as well. She has never strayed far from the music scene, starring in the Broadway hit *Smokey Joe's Café*, composing songs with her brother, Michael Gore, co-writing the Oscar-nominated *Out Here on My Own*, and keeping up a busy concert schedule across the country.

Lesley Gore did spend eight years living in California. "I would have come back sooner," she said, "but I didn't have an overcoat." But New York is the New Jersey-born Gore's home now where she lives with her partner of 23 years, jewelry designer Lois D. Sasson, on the Upper East Side.

The Village remains one of her favorite places in the city. It is where Gore's best friend, feminist writer Robin Morgan, lives. "I spend a good part of the summer practicing my grilling skills in her backyard," she says. And Bella Abzug "was my mentor in the 1970s," getting her involved in women and children's issues. Gore later leant her talents to raising money for gay and AIDS causes, continuing a lifetime of social commitment that included working in the late Robert Kennedy's 1968 presidential campaign.

We photographed Gore at Da Silvano's restaurant on Sixth Avenue, where she loves coming for birthdays or other special occasions.

Vivian Gornick

AUTHOR

Vivian Gornick, author of *Fierce Attachments*, once wrote a piece saying, "I live in the Village by default—because of all the things that it is not in contrast to the Upper West Side (bourgeois) and Upper East Side (rich)."

In the Village for forty years, she remembers it when it was "bohemia." She says, "I do not live here out of sentimental attachment to what it was when I was a girl," but for what it is today—"a neighborhood of the oddly attached."

She has seen the residents of her building on W. 12th Street go from "women right out of a Dorothy Parker story" to gay men to "people like myself, living alone, hurrying in and out of the building." Walking in the Village, "there is always a whole range of people that I can run into who populated my life-acquaintances, intimates, writers—it was always like that. The minute that I come home from anywhere else, I feel a deep sense of relief crossing 12th Street. The 'neighborhoodness' of the neighborhood is immense. The times that I do feel like I'm pleasurably in the old Village is when I walk on the streets west of Hudson. I feel a deep, secure expansiveness."

Carol Greitzer

CITY COUNCIL MEMBER

You may take for granted the charming character and unique architecture of Greenwich Village, but it would not look anything like it does today were it not for Carol Greitzer's tireless efforts in the great preservation campaigns of the 1960s.

Greitzer moved to the Village in the mid-1950s and plunged into politics, working on the local Adlai Stevenson campaign that was the precursor of the Village Independent Democrats club, which went up against the entrenched political boss Carmine De Sapio, who led the local Tamawa Club and all of Tammany Hall. She became president of VID, a district leader, and City Council Member when her colleague, Ed Koch, went to Congress in 1969.

"I wasn't the first woman elected to office in Manhattan, but in 1969 I was the only woman holding elected office in the borough," she said. And that same year, she assumed the national presidency of the National Abortion Rights Action League at a time when abortion was still illegal in the state. "After being president of VID, you can handle anything," she said.

Working with other Villagers like Jane Jacobs in the early 1960s before there was a landmarks preservation law, Greitzer played a role in saving the 1873 High Victorian Gothic Jefferson Market court house on Sixth Avenue at West 10th Street. "We got them to agree it would make a good library," she said, since the City wanted to tear it down and put up a nondescript modern building.

Greitzer also worked to get buses out of Washington Square Park and to stop Robert Moses from bulldozing the West Village and also from building the Lower Manhattan Expressway through Soho. She led the fight to keep the City from cutting a new street through houses on Bedford, Carmine and Downing Streets. Ultimately, preservationists got Greenwich Village designated an historic district.

"Once we got people mobilized for one of these campaigns, you could call on them for all the subsequent ones," she said. "We did very well. They were very exciting times."

Mel Gussow

AUTHOR AND CULTURAL WRITER

Mel Gussow has graced us with more than four decades of writing on culture—mostly theater—for *The New York Times*, *New Yorker* magazine and in books of conversations with such giants as Samuel Beckett and Tom Stoppard. He was a Guggenheim Fellow and winner of the George Jean Nathan Award for Dramatic Criticism.

Gussow's base in New York has always been Greenwich Village, where real-life dramas occur, such as the explosion of a Weather Underground bomb factory next door to his building. It is this short essay, however, that evokes happier thoughts as he recalls his building and neighborhood:

"If walls had ears, I could hear the voices of Paul and Jane Bowles and Dashiell Hammett, all of whom lived at the same time in the house I now live in. It was in the late 1940s and the Bowleses and Oliver Smith rented three floors in this Greenwich Village brownstone—Paul on the top floor with his piano under the skylight, Smith one floor below and Jane on the floor under that. Together they had a communal kitchen. And downstairs in the duplex was Hammett. Years later, Marcel Duchamp lived there. The Village, as it still is, was alive with artists.

"Moving here in the early 1960s, I cherished the quietude of the neighborhood and also took advantage of the burgeoning of the arts. At Ellen Stewart's La Mama and other theaters, Sam Shepard, Lanford Wilson, Charles Ludlum, Richard Foreman and so many others were making their first deep impressions. It was across the Village, too, that I traced the journey of Edward Albee—in his life and work—for my biography of him."

Mel Gussow died on April 29, 2005, at age 71.

Uta Hagen

ACTOR AND ACTING TEACHER

A veteran of more than 60 years in the theater, actress Uta Hagen, born in Europe, settled in Greenwich Village in 1937.

"I felt as if I had arrived in my home," she says of her first time here. When we spoke with her in 2001 she said, "There is no place that I can do my work except in New York."

Hagen's stellar acting career included playing opposite Paul Robeson in *Othello* and creating the role of Martha in Albee's *Who's Afraid of Virginia Woolf.*

After starring on Broadway with Herbert Berghof in 1947, she joined the faculty of his HB Studio where she has been teaching acting ever since. (They married in 1957 and Mr. Berghof died in 1990.) Their students are a Who's Who of the American stage—from Eli Wallach and Maureen Stapleton to Geraldine Page and George Segal to F. Murray Abraham and Whoopi Goldberg with many in between and since.

HB finally settled in Greenwich Village on Bank Street in 1959—in a move financed in part by loyal students and angels like Hume Cronyn and Jessica Tandy.

In her history of the studio, Hagen recalled that at her husband's death, "If my fervent purpose to perpetuate his life's work was to become a reality, at least as it had manifested itself on Bank Street, I had to learn what that entailed down to the grubbiest detail. For the next four months, I had labored, literally, 22 hours each day. Sometimes I wondered when my mind and body would give way. They didn't."

Uta Hagen died on January 14, 2004. The Village and the world of theater still enjoy a thriving HB.

Barry Harris

JAZZ PIANIST, COMPOSER, TEACHER

Barry Harris has memories of playing Village clubs since the 1950s that are not in the least sad. He recalls places such as the old Five Spot on West 4th at Fifth Avenue where he played with Wes Montgomery and Cecil Taylor, and the Half Note on Hudson and Spring where he saw Coltrane and Monk play.

"One special thing about that place," he remembers, "they had an old waiter—he was the most beautiful cat. There was lots of smoking, but if you took out a cigarette, he'd light it. You couldn't light it yourself—he was too fast. He took care of the whole room."

And when they were done jamming? "Interesting thing about the Village: after the joints closed (gigs get over about 4 o'clock), there was a place on MacDougal close to Bleecker. Man, let me tell you. You could go in there and have breakfast and they had everybody on the jukebox—Monk and Bird and Coleman Hawkins. It would be the best breakfast you could possibly eat, 'all jazz' listening to Bird on the juke box!"

Harris founded the Jazz Cultural Theater in the 1980s to advance the art form and lectures all over the world about it. He received an honorary degree from Northwestern University, the "Living Jazz Legacy" award from the Mid-Atlantic Arts Association and was honored by the Manhattan Borough President for his public service.

He continues to promote the classic jazz style that was developed by Charlie Parker, Dizzy Gillespie, Bud Powell, Thelonious Monk and Coleman Hawkins.

Lewis Harrison

PSYCHIC

Lewis Harrison is the Village's resident psychic and expert on haunted houses. The one on 83 West 3rd St., he says, "is very haunted. There's a haunted attic where a number of phenomenon have occurred–sounds that some could hear and others could not. There were psychic odors and cold spots. The temperature goes down when there's a ghost. There are poltergeist phenomena like pictures flying off the wall for which there are no natural explanations." He says that the house was once owned by a mobster named Bertolotti, "a friend of Joe Kennedy who used to go there. It was a strip club. He was set up in a private room."It became a fraternity house. It is quite old. Why are there ghosts there? "In the 19th century," he says, "'feeble-minded' people were often shut up in the attic. That's mostly where the noises, the voices, the cold spots and the odors were."

Kitty Carlisle Hart

ACTRESS, SINGER, ARTS ADVOCATE

Ever the quintessential uptown lady, Kitty Carlisle Hart's love for the arts nonetheless took her most everywhere, including Greenwich Village.

Born in New Orleans and schooled and trained in acting in Europe, Kitty Carlisle made her Broadway debut in *Champagne Sec* followed by her most famous feature film, *A Night at the Opera* with Allan Jones and the Marx Brothers.

More stage work followed and in 1946, she married legendary Broadway playwright and director Moss Hart. "I was very happy to be married to him," she said, "and I thought he was a genius." Moss Hart's memoir, *Act One*, is a classic. They had two children, Christopher Hart, himself a playwright, producer, and director, and Cathy Hart, a prominent physician.

Many know Kitty Carlisle for her sparkling and elegant presence as a panelist on television's *To Tell the Truth* show for many years. And she continued to work in movies (Woody Allen's *Radio Days* in 1987) and in theatre, including her one-woman shows, *My Broadway Memories* and *My Life on the Wicked Stage* that she performed throughout the country. In 1988, she published her own memoir, *Kitty*.

But it is her work on the New York State Council on Arts that may be her most enduring legacy. She was first appointed by Governor Nelson Rockefeller, then made chair by Governor Hugh Carey in 1976, and led the council until 1997. She presided over the granting of hundreds of millions of dollars to arts groups large and small throughout the state and kept convincing a sometimes-skeptical state legislature to keep funding this vital sector.

Chairing the Arts Council could require diplomacy, especially when the venue was the Village. "One day we were visiting a small exhibition in the Village to see a show that we were funding," she said. While there was nothing controversial about the council-funded exhibit, the adjoining room housed another show that would have fulfilled the worst expectations of Sen. Jesse Helms. Mrs. Hart saw the trouble spot before Mrs. John D. Rockefeller, who was on her way in, and stood at the entrance to it, telling her innocently, "There's nothing in there of any interest."

"I had to protect my constituents," Kitty Carlisle Hart confided—and well she did for more than two decades of service.

Kitty Carlisle Hart passed away on April 17, 2007, at 96.

Luther Henderson

MUSICAL DIRECTOR AND PIANIST

Luther Henderson is famous for being the musical director of Broadway's *Ain't Misbehavin'*. But "my first real job was as a pianist in George's Tavern in the Village" where he played with the Leonard Ware Trio. He also worked with singer Anita Ellis at the Bon Soir on 8th Street, the place that also gave Barbra Streisand her start. And he used to go to Marie's Crisis Café a lot with his wife and "join the gang singing at the bar."

Henderson said that "what's special about the Village is the energy, the young people going out to set the world on fire—the 'now' generation. The cast changes but the feelings remain the same. Of the legendary Village nightspots, he said, "It either works or it doesn't. The Vanguard has it. The Café Society had it. The Bon Soir. It's the people."

In 2002, he and his wife, actress/director Billie Allen, won Pioneer Awards at the Audelco "VIV" Awards. Luther Henderson died on July 28, 2003, at the age of 84. He was honored posthumously with the Jazz Masters Award from the National Endowment for the Arts in 2004.

Geoffrey Holder

ARTIST: PAINTER, DANCER, ACTOR, CHOREOGRAPHER, PHOTOGRAPHER, DESIGNER

Many artists got their start in the Village, but Geoffrey Holder was already internationally acclaimed when he sang at Art D'Lugoff's Village Gate in 1960—with Nina Simone opening for him.

Born and raised in Trinidad, Holder came to New York in the late 1940s, won a Guggenheim Fellowship to pursue his painting, danced with the Metropolitan Opera and in a Broadway show, *House of Flowers*, and acted in *Waiting for Godot*. He danced with Josephine Baker in Paris and worked with Jacques Brel (when Brel was alive and well). In Cambridge, Mass., he was part of a theater company that included Siobhan McKenna, John Gielgud, and Jason Robards. "Don't limit yourself to one thing or you will hate it," he said. "The painter has to step away from the canvas and come back to see if it is still alive."

Holder has memories of the intense artistic and intellectual scene in the Village that swirled around Russian-born experimental filmmaker Maya Deren, author of *Divine Horsemen*, an ethnography of Haiti. "She had hair teased out to here," he says stretching out his long arms, "wore peasant clothes and no shoes. She was the queen of the Village!" Through her, he met Anais Nin and Joseph Campbell and Deren's composer husband Teiji Ito. "That's why I came to the Village," he said. Lucille Lortel, another Village legend, hosted his wedding at the White Barn Theater in Westport for 500 guests.

Holder has appeared in countless films and television shows, once playing The Lion in *Androcles and the Lion* to Noel Coward's Caesar. He won the Tony Award in 1975 for directing *The Wiz* and another for designing its memorable costumes.

He lives on the cusp of the Village, just below Houston Street on Broadway, with his wife, the great dancer and professor Carmen de Lavallade. Their son, Leo, is a graphic artist.

"I will always be a child," Holder said of his approach to life and art. "The day you are a man, you're dead."

Celeste Holm

ACTRESS AND CIVIC ACTIVIST

You may have been lucky enough to see Celeste Holm create the role of Ado Annie in *Oklahoma* on Broadway in the 1940s. You may know her for her Oscar-winning performance in *Gentleman's Agreement* in 1947, or for her unforgettable turn in the classic *All About Eve* as Karen, the best friend of Margo Channing (played by Bette Davis). And you will recall her, too, for the countless stage, television and film roles thereafter.

But Holm has also been a spokesperson for UNICEF, a member of the National Arts Council, a winner of the Ellis Island Medal of Honor—and she was knighted by King Olav of Norway. Central Park would not be what it is today were it not for her work in the cause of saving and restoring it.

In earlier years, Greenwich Village was her home, including a place at 39 East 10th St. and another at 14 Fifth Ave. In the latter, Holm recalled that she occupied "the drawing room of the old Rhinelander mansion, once the most eminent family in New York. My bedroom had been the foyer of the building and I had such a sense of history there. It had nineteen-foot ceilings… but I gave it up to go to Hollywood. How I wish I hadn't, I'd still be there."

Richard Howard

POET, TRANSLATOR, CRITIC, TEACHER

Richard Howard has lived in the Village for more than 30 years, now on Waverly Place but for many years on West 12th Street He shares his book-lined apartment with his French bulldog, Gide. "It's good for a dog to have a single syllable name," he said. "The next one will be Dude."

While he is from Cleveland and went to school at Columbia at a time—the 1950s—in Morningside Heights when "you had to walk a mile for a lemon," he was always attracted to the Village. Now, he said, his friends live all over New York, but the Village is where he continues to want to make his home. "I'm used to it," he said, "like the fact that most of the time the buildings are low enough to see the sky. I walk the dog four times a day in the park. Those are very valuable moments."

Howard is a distinguished poet, translator of French writers from Stendhal to Barthes, critic and professor. "I've taught all over," he said, "and don't despair anymore when someone says they are going to be working in a place like Mississippi," suggesting that some of the creative excitement once associated with the Village has penetrated into pockets throughout America.

Howard has received numerous honors for his poetry and translations, including the Pulitzer Prize in 1970 for his third collection, *Untitled Subjects* in 1970. He was Poet Laureate of New York from 1993-95.

Here he shares a poem set in the West Village from his *Inner Voices, selected poems, 1963-2003* (Farrar, Straus, Giroux, New York):

Among the Missing reprinted with permission of the poet

Know me? I am the ghost of Gansevoort Pier.
  Out of the Trucks, beside the garbage scow
  where rotten pilings form a sort of prow,
I loom, your practiced shadow, waiting here

For celebrants who cease to come my way,
  though mine are limbs as versatile as theirs
  and eyes as vagrant. Odd that no one cares
to ogle me now where I, as ever, lay

myself out, all my assets and then some,
  weather permitting. Is my voice so faint?
  Can't you hear me over the river's complaint?
Too dark to see me? Have you all become

ghosts? What earthly good is that? I want
  incarnate lovers hungry for my parts,
  longing hands and long-since-lonely hearts!
It is your living bodies I must haunt,

and while the Hudson hauls its burdens past,
  having no hosts to welcome or repel
  disclosures of the kind I do so well,
I with the other ghosts am laid at last.

Kim Hunter

ACTRESS

Kim Hunter, a stage and film legend who will never be forgotten as Stella in *A Streetcar Named Desire*, had lived all over the city as a young actress. She once took over a lease from Tennessee Williams on the East Side when he left for Europe. But then she moved to Grove Street when she married Bob Emmett in 1951. Later she emigrated to Central Park West for larger quarters after the birth of daughter Catherine and the impending birth of son Sean, but was drawn back to the Village and Commerce Street within six months.

"It took all three of us to realize that we liked the Village much better," she said, "and that the Upper West Side was not nearly as good. We didn't like the tall buildings or the shopping."

At the time of our interview she said, "We've now lived here on Commerce for 46 years—longer than I've lived anywhere." For years, she was involved in the BBC—not the British Broadcasting Corporation, but the Bedford, Barrow, Commerce block association where she cooked up her legendary and huge carrot cake for their annual Ye Olde Village Fair in mid-May.

Kim Hunter died on September 11, 2002, at the age of 79.

Anne Jackson
ACTOR, WRITER, TEACHER

Eli Wallach
ACTOR AND PHOTOGRAPHER

Acting giants Eli Wallach and Anne Jackson attended the Neighborhood Playhouse School of Theatre in the 1940s (although not together) and are still associated with it. They studied with Lee Strasberg in the late '40s, Jackson also with Herbert Berghof. She teaches now at HB Studio on Bank Street. They met doing *This Property is Condemned*, a two-hander by Tennessee Williams at the Hudson Street Equity Library Theatre. They walked to it from where Jackson was living at 43 Fifth Ave. in a room that was originally "maid's quarters—no light, no view and $35 a month." They talked of Ben Smirnoff's drugstore, Whitney Chemist, from those days where "he gave us breakfast, he treated actors well." Wallach recalled rehearsing in Burgess Meredith's Village place. Jackson remembered rehearsing *Major Barbara*, which they did on Broadway, in Charles Laughton's apartment on 10th Street "We got Uta Hagen her apartment on Waverly Place," Jackson said. "It really was a village."

Wallach and Jackson have done stage work from Broadway to the London's West End. Wallach won a Tony for *The Rose Tattoo* in 1951. They also worked the Village, doing *The Scarecrow* at the Theatre de Lys (now the Lucille Lortel) with Patricia Neal and James Dean, then an understudy. They returned there to do *Brecht on Brecht* in the late '60s.

They both picked up Obie awards for their performances in *The Tiger* and *The Typists* in 1963 at the Phoenix Theatre on Second Avenue and 8th Street.

Jackson played Village legend Bella Abzug in a 1987 TV movie of Shirley MacLaine's autobiographical *Out on a Limb*. Wallach won an Emmy for *The Poppy is Also a Flower* in 1967.

They returned to the Village in 2001 to do Anne Meara's *Down the Garden Path* at the Minetta Lane Theater. "It became a family affair with our daughter Roberta in it as well," Jackson said. Daughter Katherine Wallach is also an actress. Son Peter, born in the Village, is a film animator. Jackson and Wallach are still addicted to the sherbet cones on Bleecker Street.

Rose James

POET AND SOCIAL WORKER

Rose James has been a fixture in the Village since 1967. But she is sensitive to the people we see every day for a long time and who then disappear—the homeless.

"Every time I went to the Sloan's on Mercer and West 3rd," she said, "there was this young, attractive black woman there collecting cans with two other homeless, one her boyfriend.

"I'd always talk to her and she called me 'Mom' and said she was trying to dress like I did. She would say, 'I'm trying to get myself together,' but she was alcoholic and it didn't seem likely.

"I offered to take her to Judson Church with me, but she would say, 'I don't feel like it today.'

"One Sunday morning I heard sirens and later when I went outside, there was blood on the sidewalk where she had fallen after a seizure. She got better and went back to the streets, but this happened two or three times until she finally went home to North Carolina where I'm from originally.

"Turned out her father was a minister there. I thought she would recover down South, but her boyfriend told me she died a short time later. She was only 37, young enough to be my daughter. It was tremendously sad. Touched me so much."

Margo Jefferson

CULTURAL CRITIC, TEACHER, PERFORMER

When Margo Jefferson won the Pulitzer Prize for Criticism in 1995, it was no surprise. Her insightful writing on theatre and books graced the pages of *The New York Times* for years. She has also written for *Newsweek*, *Vogue*, *The Village Voice Literary Supplement*, *Harper's* and *O, the Oprah Magazine* among other publications.

Living in the West Village since 1974, Jefferson said, has allowed her "to live somewhat apart from the pressures of following styles and what is 'in.' Not that there aren't plenty of well-off people—still there is a myth and reality here about thinking individually and living the way you want to and living the life of the mind."

Jefferson grew up in Chicago and once lived on the Upper West Side, but now she says she "can't imagine living anywhere else in the City. Not that I would ever leave New York, but I like the trees and the odd views in the Village—something that is a bit of a retreat from New York."

In addition to her work for *The Times*, Jefferson has been a senior fellow at Columbia's National Journalism Arts Program and an artist-in-residence at Anna Deveare Smith's Institute for the Arts and Civic Dialogue, now in the Village at New York University. At the Cherry Lane Theatre in the West Village, she performed *50 Minutes with Harriet and Phyllis* with her niece, Francesca Harper. And her solo *60 Minutes in Negroland* —a series of monologues that looked "at the transition between the old world of the black bourgeoisie and the changed black world of the 1960s"—was done at the Cherry Lane and at the Culture Project in the East Village.

In 2006, her book *On Michael Jackson* was published. She continues to teach at Columbia and The New School.

Diana Kan

ARTIST

Diana Kan has gone from displaying her watercolors at the Washington Square Outdoor Art Exhibit in the 1950s to being today a National Academician at the National Academy of Design and a fellow of the Royal Society of Arts in Britain with works in the permanent collections at the Metropolitan Museum of Art, the Philadelphia Museum of Art and the Taiwan Museum of Art. *Eastern Spirit, Western World*, a book of her paintings, is also the title of a documentary on her life shown on PBS. Since 1999, she has been a member of the New York City Cultural Affairs Advisory Committee.

Hong Kong native Diana Kan's art is rooted in her homeland, but much of her life has been spent on West 9th Street between Fifth and Sixth avenues. "There's something about the block that speaks to me of China," she said. Indeed, a century ago, the Chinese Consul General lived in a brownstone where her apartment building now stands. "If I had to choose where to live, Greenwich Village is my first choice," she said. "Everyone knows one another."

In front of her building, a tree honors the memory of her late husband Paul Schwartz, whom she met at the Art Students League. The block itself holds memories; for example, of late poet Marianne Moore, a neighbor. "She and my husband had good times talking about baseball."

Kan has also used her work in the service of her community, writing art reviews and contributing illustrations to the weekly newspaper *The Villager* for many years. "I shall never forget that once upon a time I was an outdoor artist," she said. She continues to help out with that spring and fall exhibit. In 1997, she won the Gold Medal of Honor from the Village's Salmagundi Club for her vibrant landscapes, flowers and people.

Lainie Kazan

SINGER AND ACTRESS

"My very first theatre piece was done in the Village in 1959, *Leave it to Jane* by Jerome Kern," said Lainie Kazan. She was walking through the Village with a girlfriend from school and they saw an "Auditions Today" sign outside the Sheridan Square Playhouse.

"She wanted to, I didn't," she said. "She auditioned. I didn't. The producer asked me if I could sing. I said, 'A little.' I sang and they hired me. They didn't hire her. The show ran for two years. George Segal was in it, too. I made $17.95 a week. My whole life was down there. It was when the Village was really happening. Bob Dylan, Joni Mitchell. It was the beginning of the folk era."

And from those Village roots, Lainie Kazan is still going strong.

Edward I. Koch

FORMER MAYOR OF THE CITY OF NEW YORK

During his mayoralty from 1978-89, Ed Koch was part of many public gatherings in the Village where he lived both before and after a stint in Gracie Mansion. But he remembered a private moment with a world legend.

"During my administration," he said, "Mother Theresa opened an AIDS hospice. She told me, 'My greatest joy is when I am able to bring a reconciliation between parents and young men suffering from AIDS. Very often people who are dying ask me to sit with them. They take my hands and put my fingers on their lesions. Then they ask me for a ticket to heaven. I always give them that ticket.' She will be sorely missed."

Connie Kopelov

FEMINIST LABOR ORGANIZER AND EDUCATOR

Phyllis Siegel

BOOKKEEPER AND ACCOUNTANT

Connie Kopelov and Phyllis Siegel met in the SAGE Room at the Lesbian and Gay Community Center on 13th Street, but didn't really connect until a SAGE dance at P.S. 1 on Hudson Street.

"SAGE had a holiday social on a cold night in 1987," Connie recalled. "I was living in New Jersey at the time and was looking forward to moving to the Village," said Phyllis. "We got to talking with each other and got up to dance," said Connie, and started teaching each other dance steps including "the Shuffle, the Lindy."

Phyllis added, "We've been dancing ever since." They also talked about marching through the Village on Gay Pride Day every June. "The crowds are so wonderful to us in SAGE," they said.

While no longer a couple and now both retired, the women are still close friends and maintain their commitment to SAGE and its work of serving gay and lesbian older people and advocating for their rights.

Larry Kramer

AUTHOR AND ACTIVIST

David Webster

ARCHITECT

During the initial terrible moments of the AIDS crisis, Larry Kramer convened a meeting in his place that led to the formation of Gay Men's Health Crisis (GMHC). It was at his place too that later in the '80s, ACT UP activities were plotted—another response begun by Larry to the epidemic.

Larry has lived in the same Village apartment for 28 years, and when we interviewed him with architect/designer David Webster in 1999 they were busy at work transforming the place once again to one where, after many years apart from each other, they would live together. Making it, as David, who is on the left in the photo, said, "into a peaceful calm interior."

The two have been together at this writing for 17 years—four on-again/off-again years in the mid-70s—and now for the past 13 years.

Stanley Kunitz

POET, TEACHER, GARDENER

We had the privilege of meeting with Stanley Kunitz, twice Poet Laureate of the United States, just weeks before his death at 100 on May 14, 2006, in his Greenwich Village apartment. Born in Worcester, Massachusetts, in 1905 and a graduate of Harvard, he divided most of his adult life between New York, where he was a founder of Poets House at 72 Spring St., and Provincetown, where he co-founded the Fine Arts Work Center—reflecting his commitment to bringing poets together and helping emerging poets.

His apartment on West 12th Street was his second on the street, the first having had a "wonderful garden" and this one with a greenhouse terrace and where he stained his study's parquet floor green. Just after college, he had lived on 9th Street for a time.

He shared his last home with his wife, Elise Asher, "an incredible artist and poet," he said, until her death in 2004. The apartment contained many art works by her and a chair given to him by their friend e.e. cummings who famously lived over on Patchin Place.

Kunitz recalled earlier days in the Village. "The rents were so low," he said. "It was easier for a young artist to live here then than it is now."

Kunitz taught, among other places, at Bennington College, the Village's New School for Social Research and for 30 years at Columbia University. He received the Pulitzer Prize in 1959 for his third collection, *Selected Poems 1928-1958*." He was presented with numerous other honors, including the National Book Award, the Bollingen Prize and the Robert Frost Medal. "Poetry is the most indelible testimony we have of the adventures of the spirit," he once wrote.

This is a selection from his last book, *The Wild Braid: A Poet Reflects on a Century in the Garden* (W.W. Norton, 2005) written with poet Genine Lentine and with photographs by Marnie Crawford Samuelson. It is a fitting memorial to his life and work:

"When you look back on a lifetime and think of what has been given to the world by your presence, your fugitive presence, inevitably you think of your art, whatever it may be, as the gift you have made to the world in acknowledgement of the gift you have been given, which is the life itself. And I think the world tends to forget that this is the ultimate significance of the body of work each artist produces. That work is not an expression of the desire for praise or recognition, or prizes, but the deepest manifestation of your gratitude for the gift of life."

Bettye Lane

PHOTOGRAPHER

For more than thirty years, Bettye Lane, a longtime resident of the West Village, has been on the front lines of some of the momentous social changes of our times, not with a protest sign or bullhorn, but with her camera. Her photography has focused primarily on civil rights, the anti-war movement, the women's movement, and the fight for lesbian and gay rights. Her photos have appeared in scores of documentaries and been published in more than 70 books and newspapers here and around the world. They are also featured in the archives of the Smithsonian Institution, the United Nations, the New York Public Library, and the National Museum of Women in the Arts in Washington, D.C. The U.S. Postal Service included one of her photos in the "Celebrate the Century" stamp series for the year 2000.

In her Westbeth apartment, Lane is surrounded by images from the turbulent movements of the 1960s, '70s, and '80s. ("It got quieter in the '90s," she said.) Getting these pictures wasn't easy. She was once hit in the back of the head with a billy club by a cop. She recalled an anti-war protest in Washington Square Park in 1974 where she was slipped a note saying that someone was going to knock over the press stand. None of the TV and still photographers bailed out, "though the movement people kept folks back." And she was a few feet from mobster Joe Colombo when he was shot in Columbus Circle in 1971 at an Italian-American rally.

"I loved protests when they were *really* protesting," she said, "when they were there because they were not being heard. I photographed the human condition and the human spirit."

Lane got her start at the Harvard University News Office, which let her go to Boston University's School of Communications to learn photography. She bought her first Leica from Michael Rockefeller for $50. She went to New York to do still work for CBS ("I was flattered and terrified," she said), but struggled because most companies were not hiring women for this work in the early 1960s.

She got her break photographing a protest at the UN in 1966 ("I always got into the middle of a demonstration," she said) and met the photo editor at the *National Observer* in Washington to which she contributed for years. At the height of the anti-war movement, "there were sometimes four or five demos a day," she said.

Bettye Lane said that "living in the Village is living" and that her end of the Village is the best part. "I know my storekeepers, druggist, bank people. You don't feel isolated here. There is also so much stimulation—the arts, galleries, bookstores, theater and architecture. I'll never leave!"

Arthur Laurents

PLAYWRIGHT, SCREENWRITER, DIRECTOR

Even if you've never been to St. Luke's Place in the Village, you've likely seen it in the movies as the quintessential "Village" block. This is the street where Mayor Jimmy Walker—and his mistress, Betty Compton—lived in the 1920s. It also happens to be where Arthur Laurents and his partner Tom Hatcher found a home in 1961.

"When I was a kid in Brooklyn, my dream was to have an apartment in the Village for $150," Laurents said in the parlor of his townhouse. "Now here I am in this house." They were shown the place on a Wednesday and were given a day to decide (they'd asked for a week). They have stayed put ever since. "If you see a place you like," he advised, "grab it and stay."

Growing up, the Village represented "freedom of all kinds," he said, "a sort of bohemia. I still think it is the only real neighborhood in New York."

In his rich life in the theatre and film, Laurents has written musicals from *West Side Story* and *Gypsy* (which he later also directed with Angela Lansbury and Tyne Daly) to *Hallelujah Baby!* earning a Tony award. His direction of *La Cage Aux Folles* also garnered him a Tony. His screenplays include: *Anastasia*, starring Ingrid Bergman: *Rope*, directed by Alfred Hitchcock; Golden Globe-winning *The Turning Point*, with Ann Bancroft and Shirley MacLaine, and *The Way We Were*, with Barbra Streisand and Robert Redford.

His autobiography, *Original Story by Arthur Laurents: A Memoir of Broadway and Hollywood*, came out in 2001.

Ralph Lee

THEATRICAL MASK MAKER, VILLAGE HALLOWEEN PARADE CREATOR

Ralph Lee may not be a familiar face, but the images of his masks and puppets are, whether you are a theatergoer, have attended the Village Halloween Parade or have seen *Saturday Night Live* on TV (where his memorable Land Shark appeared less than 24 hours after the producers asked for it).

Lee grew up in Vermont, where he started making puppets as a teenager, and came to New York in the late 1950s to pursue a life in the theater. He landed a role in Camus's *Caligula* on Broadway with Colleen Dewhurst where his one line was, "I summon thee, O Death!" It was the costumer for that show, Ray Diffen, who got him interested in that end of the business. He did masks for *The Tempest* in Stratford and the rest is history—much of it in the Village.

He worked with Joe Chaikin's Open Theater for many years, but also designed for Julian Beck, Shari Lewis and Eric Hawkins. "I'm most proud of my work for Hawkins," he said, "because he took all the visual elements of a show very seriously. He wouldn't start rehearsing until he had the masks."

In 1970, Lee was one of the first tenants admitted to the then-new Westbeth artists complex in the Village, then a project of the Kaplan Fund. It was from there that he started the Village Halloween Parade in 1974, at first co-sponsored by the Theater for a New City and its director, Crystal Field. Ralph Lee's idea was a parade that got the community involved as it wound its serpentine way from Westbeth on the Hudson to Washington Square Park—"the only parade in New York that was strictly crosstown," he noted. He didn't just bring his puppets to the streets, but staged things on balconies and fire escapes along the route.

"My vision of Halloween was a very traditional one—ghosts and witches and pumpkins," he said. "In Vermont, it is a seasonal holiday that acknowledges the movement from summer to winter. Our parade reminded people in the city—detached from nature—what was happening in the natural world. We brought big swamp grasses in from Jersey and created "a sea of foliage."

Lee himself used to walk along with the parade. One year he noticed a teenager buying eggs in a deli on the route and putting the ammo into his coat pockets. Rather than let these dangerous missiles fly, he gave the kid a big bear hug, smashing the eggs right in the kid's coat!

The parade outgrew the Village's sidestreets and had to be moved to Sixth Avenue. Lee, who no longer runs the parade, and bids his creation well, wishes communities throughout the region had developed their own, interactive neighborhood Halloween parades rather than making the Village's such a gargantuan production.

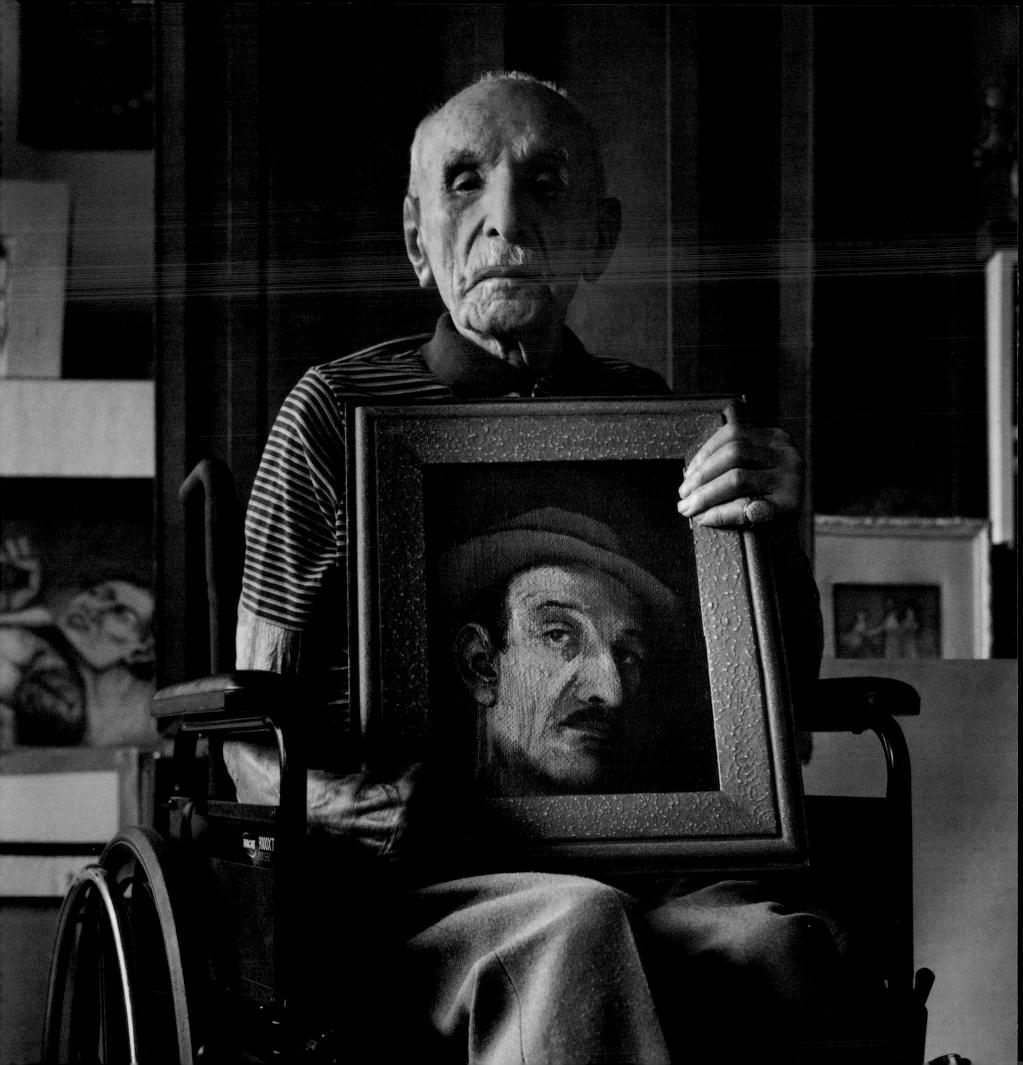

Alfred Levitt

ARTIST

Alfred Levitt, 105 years old when we interviewed him in 1999, emigrated from Russia in 1911 and first lived in the Village in 1913. "It was an oasis for men and women who seek creative expression," he says. "They formed a group whose lives were dedicated to seek and produce expression of what the Village offered."

Levitt remembers Jack London ("a revolutionary American writer and very able man"). He studied with Robert Henri and Hans Hoffman. On West 14th Street, he lived downstairs from Marcel Duchamp, painter of *Nude Descending a Staircase*, and remembers him as a man who "craved immediate recognition." He knew the radicals of the day including John Reed.

"At the time it was almost a necessity to espouse political change," he said.

His vivid paintings include 25 in the permanent collection of the Metropolitan Museum of Art and 20 at Mary Washington College Galleries in Virginia. His famous *Paysage Provencal*, a watercolor (1950) was featured in an Ellis Island Immigration Museum exhibit of his works in 1998—"Alfred Levitt: Through these Portals."

For all of his artistic achievement, Levitt's fondest memory of the Village, where he still lived at the time of his death, dates back to when dances were held under the Washington Square arch every Sunday. "They had a band and young girls and boys came around to dance. I met my wife, Gertrude, at a concert in 1924."

He passed away in May of 2000.

Al Lewis

ACTOR, POLITICAL ACTIVIST, RADIO HOST, RACONTEUR

He presided over Grandpa's Italian restaurant, named for his famous *Munster's* TV character, on Bleecker Street for eight years. Al Lewis's memories of the Village, however, go back a lot longer.

Lewis recalled a 24-hour cafeteria on Sixth Avenue south of 8th Street: "I met a boy named Allen Ginsburg, sat with Joe Gould who was writing the history of the world, e.e. cummings, Dorothy Day—all the radicals of the day." And he remembered the Savannah Club where female impersonators performed. "It was the first place anyone saw Tiny Tim. I brought him there. He was a fan of mine."

There was an "unpleasant" side to the Village of the 1950s and '60s, Lewis said, with "the sadistic beatings of gay people that went on; the police were watching and laughing every night when the clubs broke on 8th Street as wolf packs would beat them senseless." Al, ever the champion of the downtrodden, decided to do something about it. "I had a number of friends," he said, "who if they came to your door and you opened it, they would block the sun, all around 6'5" and 270-300 lbs. and professional athletes. I told them what was happening to the gays and they went insane. So we went down near the Bon Soir around closing time and here came the wolf pack to beat up the gays. My five guys sent all these thugs to the hospital." Why were his friends so protective of Village gay people? "They just didn't like bully tactics," Al said. "It's un-American."

Al Lewis died on February 3, 2006, with his age much in dispute. What was indisputable was his lifelong commitment to social justice.

Jimmy Lou

PAINTER

Jimmy Lou spent almost all of his life in Chinatown, which he hardly ever left except to meet his wife Fay in China. It was a traditional arranged marriage that has lasted more than 50 years. "So many people who make their own choice are only married a year or two," he says.

Slowed down a bit by the cerebral palsy that he has had since childhood, Mr. Lou moved to the Village Nursing Home in 1990. "I had never been to the Village until I lived here," Lou says. "I don't miss Chinatown."

Jimmy Lou has himself become a Village legend, known for rolling out his wheelchair to the corner of W. 12th and Hudson, "my sunshine corner," where he has struck up relationships with scores of "strangers." "You can always talk to people here and they talk to you," he says, "and lots of them are pretty actresses to look at." He says that his wife doesn't mind. "She says, 'What makes you happy, makes me happy.'"

Lou, who has two children and two grandchildren, is also famous for his vibrant water colors, an art he picked up only after moving to his new home. "Nobody taught me. I never painted before," he says. "I give most of my paintings away."

Darlene Love

SINGER AND ACTOR

The New York Times once wrote, "Darlene Love's thunderbolt voice is as embedded in the history of Rock-and-Roll as Eric Clapton's guitar or Bob Dylan's lyrics." Born in Los Angeles with a minister father, Love sang in choir. "I wanted to sing like Marion Anderson," she said.

Love's first group was The Blossoms, recorded by Phil Spector. Thereafter she sang lead vocals for many of the greatest hits of the 1960s, although her name was never credited on tunes such as *He's a Rebel* and *He's Sure the Boy I Love*. Love sang and arranged backup vocals for as many as 200 of the era's songs sung by the likes of the Righteous Brothers, the Mamas and the Papas, Jan and Dean and many others.

Her legendary singing voice remains powerful today. What is the secret? "When working," she said, "I don't talk to anybody. Talking is harder on the voice than anything. I drink eight to ten glasses of water a day and drink no hard alcohol, though some wine. And I get a lot of rest."

When she first took her solo act to New York in 1984, it was at the Village's Bottom Line. "It was scary," she said. "I wondered who was going to come and see me." But soon she discovered: "In New York, they're either for you or against you. I'm blessed—they're with me here. I had thought people in New York were not friendly, but they're the friendliest in the world." She has also played CBGB's in the East Village and Rainbow and Stars uptown.

Love moved to the New York area permanently in 1984 and has no desire to move back to California. "People here feel they know you," she said on a visit to Joe's Pub in the Village's Public Theater. "In other cities, you're just working."

Her annual staged Christmas show is now a holiday staple in New York as is her regular Decenber performance on *David Letterman*.

David Margulies

ACTOR AND DIRECTOR

David Margulies played Appopolous, the eccentric Village landlord and painter, in *Wonderful Town* on Broadway, but this accomplished New York-born actor has real Village roots. He once lived at 52 MacDougal Street in a tenement apartment with the bathroom in the kitchen and remembers working the Player's Theater on the same street, as well as the Orpheum on Second Avenue and Circle in the Square on Bleecker Street. Now in Hell's Kitchen, he still returns to the Village to get his hair cut at Frank's on Thompson Street, stopping in DoJo's at West 4th and Mercer for a bite.

In his college days, it was Fellin's restaurant on Thompson Street where he hung out with the avant garde. "It wasn't one scene," he said. "There was a Trotskyist table and a table for anyone who was alone, where an exotic gay bohemian man sat. Italians drank grappa at the bar. There was a bocce court out back." At 3 Washington Square North, a studio building, he remembers seeing artist Edward Hopper, "tall and fierce," who lived there, at a play reading "with his beautiful wife, Jo." Margulies also recalled, "My cousin Paul had a studio there and painted my portrait often,"

During the Vietnam Era, he conducted theatrical workshops on Bleecker Street, experimenting with new techniques with a "lot of America's best young actors." He noted, "In Rip Torn's Sanctuary Theater at Greenwich House, I appeared in Rip's Torn's *Hamlet* as well as Murray Schisgal's *The Flatulist*, a largely unknown comic masterpiece."

On Broadway, Margulies has performed in everything from *The Iceman Cometh* in 1973 to *Angels in America* in the 1990s and one of the leads in Herb Gardner' *Conversations with My Father*. Regionally, he has been Sir Anthony Absolute in *The Rivals* at Hartford Stage, in *She Stoops to Conquer* at the Long Wharf, been *King Lear* in Buffalo and done Arthur Miller's *The Price* at the Guthrie. He has directed at the Public Theater including one of their Central Park productions. Among his many screen roles, this quintessential New Yorker has memorably played the mayor of New York in the movie *Ghostbusters* and Tony Soprano's lawyer, Neil Mink, on *The Sopranos* on television.

Frank McCourt

AUTHOR AND TEACHER

Long before he became, as he puts it, "PulitzerprizewinningauthorFrankMcCourt," he was Frankie McCourt. He was born in Brooklyn, but spent his "miserable Irish Catholic childhood" in Limerick. He returned to New York—as did his brothers Malachy, Mike, and Alphie—and lived in every borough, including stints in the Village at 46 Downing St. and on Carmine Street where he remembers "the kids playing stickball in the street with eyes in the back of their heads for cars." He applied to New York University on a whim one day in Washington Square Park, but kept at it, and worked his way through college.

McCourt taught for thirty years at different New York City schools: McKee Vocational on Staten Island, and, in Manhattan, the High School of Fashion Industries, Seward Park High School and Stuyvesant High School where he taught the last 18 years of his career. He calls teaching "the best thing I ever did."

He also haunted the watering holes of the Village from the White Horse with the Clancy Brothers to McSorley's and the Old Town Bar where he is pictured here, just to the north on E. 18th. "I know where the bodies are buried," he says.

McCourt said that the now departed Lion's Head on Christopher Street was "my home away from home from 1966 to '96. I was there on opening night." It eventually became home to many of the city's top writers and journalists, including Norman Mailer, Pete Hamill and Dennis Duggan.

"I was only a teacher," McCourt once said in an interview for the Academy of Achievement. "And I only had one dream: to have my book jacket framed on that wall." A few months before the Lion's Head closed in October 1996, Mike Riordan, the owner, invited him in for a drink. After toasting him, Riordan said, "Turn around."

"And I turned around," McCourt said, "and there was my framed book jacket. That was it. For me, that was the Nobel Prize. To be on the wall of the Lion's Head." He added, "As soon as I do anything, the publication or the pub closes down. If I send a short story to a magazine, they publish it and then they go out of business. But not in the case of *Angela's Ashes*."

McCourt followed his best-selling memoir with another, *'Tis*, about his life in America and in 2005, *Teacher Man*, about all those years in the classroom.

Malachy McCourt

ACTOR, AUTHOR, SOCIAL COMMENTATOR

Malachy McCourt is celebrated for many things, not least of which is being the first to get the word "hell" in the telephone directory. This was in 1975 when he was running a saloon called The Bells of Hell on West 13th Street. When he asked for a listing, the phone company told him it was a four-letter word. He met resistance at every level of the bureaucracy, despite pointing out that the bible was full of references to hell. He didn't get his listing until columnist Earl Wilson wrote it up.

McCourt recounts this tale sitting at The White Horse Tavern, one of the places, he points out, where Dylan Thomas drank himself to death. McCourt says he himself gave up the sauce "for the sake of the wife and kidneys."

He remembers lean times in the Village, living in a coldwater flat on Downing Street in the 1950s for $25 a month. "It was set up for gas, but there was no gas stove. Con Edison sent a bill for gas anyway and I sent it back marked 'deceased.' They then cut off the lights as well."

McCourt is known through his writing, from his autobiography *A Monk Swimming* to his *West Side Spirit* column "Sez I to Myself" to his latest political work, *Bush Lies in State*. Born in Brooklyn and raised in Ireland, he came back to New York in 1952 and survived through all kinds of jobs before working in radio, TV, movies and the stage, including *A Couple of Blackguards* with his brother, Frank. He is "happily married to Diana, is the proud father of five children, and the grandfather of three."

McCourt ran for governor of New York on the Green Party line in 2006.

Fred W. McDarrah

PHOTOGRAPHER

Here's a picture of Fred W. McDarrah, but it is the evocative images he made while on the other side of the camera, many of them of people and places in the Village, that give him legendary status. He took those unique photographs since the end of World War II when he settled on MacDougal Street. "Those were the days when the San Remo was the great literary bar and everyone went there," he said. He had wanted to become a magazine writer, but he soon returned to the photography that he had started in the Army.

In 1956, he was walking across Sheridan Square and ran into Norman Mailer, Ed Fancher and Dan Wolf who said, "McDarrah, we're starting a newspaper." That was the beginning of the *Village Voice*, for which "he was a contributor from the start, becoming a staff photographer in 1959, then picture editor soon after. He remained consulting picture editor, more than four decades later.

"I don't think there is any other place in the world to live," he said of the Village. "The beats, the artists, gays, the '60s, the music scene—all of it contributed to the education of Fred McDarrah and to my collection of photographs. Most of the stuff I did without determination or agenda," he said. He and his wife Gloria, who partnered in his work, were married in 1960, and it was their children who pushed him to pull his pictures together for books. He has done several. He has many photos of places that no longer exist in the city, from the Washington Market to the Wall Street area, many of which formed the core of a book called *New York in the 1960s*. "I just liked the architecture," he said.

Fred McDarrah died in 2007.

Dr. Erline Perkins McGriff

PROFESSOR OF NURSING AT NYU

Dr. Erline Perkins McGriff a distinguished professor of nursing at New York University, pioneered with Dr. Pat Hurley in 1985 a massive program educating tens of thousands of health care providers about AIDS.

"I'm still working full time," she said at 70, "but when people ask when I will retire, I say it is not in my vocabulary. The University has been my family for 31 years."

In her three decades in the Village, she says, "I've experienced the loss of many friends and colleagues to AIDS. I just hope and pray that there will be a cure." She will never leave the Village. "Where else on earth can you go around the block and have gone around the world? rarely go uptown. And I don't cook, because you have the choice of whatever you want here." Her favorite is Ennio and Michael's, "right here around the corner. It's like my dining room. There are days when I've had lunch and dinner there. I'd have breakfast there if I could."

Don't let Erline McGriff's courtly Virginia manner fool you. She once served on the University Senate and was told she would be bored to death. "They were debating giving domestic partner benefits to same-sex partners, and I was appalled at senators who said we would ruin our reputation. I told them they had to change their way of thinking."

Terrence McNally

PLAYWRIGHT, LIBRETTIST, SCREENWRITER, PRODUCER

Terrence McNally first visited New York with his family at age 6 from Corpus Christi, Texas, and saw Ethel Merman in *Annie Get Your Gun*. At age 12, on another visit, he saw Gertrude Lawrence in *The King and I* a few weeks before she died. He moved to the city in 1956 to attend Columbia University and soon moved to Greenwich Village:

"This quiet corner of the West Village means a lot to me," he wrote. "My first apartment in New York, when I was a junior at Columbia, was just around the corner at 85 Barrow Street. The Blue Mill Restaurant was where I ate out 99 percent of the time and I ate out a lot. The Cherry Lane Theatre is where I first heard a professional actor speak my lines at the Barr-Wilder-Albee Playwrights Unit. It was Estelle Parsons and the play was called *This Side of the Door*. It was very intense. Next to the theatre was the Cherry Lane Bar, the first gay bar I can remember dancing in. We did stuff like The Madison—"Line Dancing" we called it; you weren't allowed to actually touch your partner. In those days, the subway at Sheridan Square became an express at 42nd Street and you could get up to Columbia in 15 minutes. The trains ran a lot more often, too. When I graduated from Columbia I decided to give a cocktail party for some of my fellow graduates and their parents. It was a 5th floor walkup and one of my friend's father had a heart attack on the 3rd floor landing. That's when I quickly decided to move the party to the Blue Mill downstairs. They were very accommodating."

McNally is one of the most important and successful playwrights of our time. He had a play, *And Things that Go Bump in the Night*, on Broadway at 25. His Broadway hit, *The Ritz*, became a feature film. He won Obies for *Bad Habits*, *Frankie and Johnny in the Clair de Lune* (which also became a film), and *The Lisbon Traviata* with Nathan Lane. His TV drama, *Andre's Mother*, starring Sada Thompson and Richard Thomas as the mother and surviving partner of a gay man who died of AIDS, brought an Emmy. He twice won the Tony Award for best play, for *Love! Valour! Compassion!* (also a film) and *Master Class* starring Zoe Caldwell, and twice for best book of a musical, for *Kiss of the Spider Woman* and *Ragtime*. He has another Broadway hit with his libretto for *The Full Monty*. And his plays with the Manhattan Theater Club, including *A Perfect Ganesh* and *Corpus Christi,* further demonstrate his extraordinary range. He wrote the libretto for an opera version of *Dead Man Walking*.

"You can't write about what you haven't experienced," McNally once said, "and there is so much is this city that is interesting." But he also admitted, "I'm not a New Yorker, I'm from Texas and I draw on that stuff. I still feel like a tourist here, but I don't want to live anywhere else."

David McReynolds

PEACE ACTIVIST AND POLITICAL LEADER

"I came to New York from Los Angeles in 1956 because I was a young radical and this is where young radicals go," said David McReynolds, who first worked at *Liberation Magazine* on Christopher Street, right across from the Theatre De Lys (now the Lucille Lortel) where he saw Lotte Lenya in *The Threepenny Opera*.

"The exciting part of the job was that the editors were radical pacifists—Dave Dellinger, Roy Finch, A. J. Muste, Bayard Rustin and Sid Lens. It was the time of the civil rights movement and Bayard would often be on the phone to Martin Luther King, Jr. We met every single Wednesday at 4 p.m., broke for dinner at 6, and then came back to work until 10."

He recalls a particularly heated argument in the office about whether pacifists should support the calling up of the National Guard to enforce a desegregation order in Little Rock, as well as sharp divisions over Cuba. "I usually sided with Bayard and AJ," he said.

In 1960, McReynolds began work at the War Resisters League as their field secretary, speaking to students and organizing the mass protests against the Civil Defense drills, which were ended after 1961. He also became one of the leaders of the Vietnam peace movement, traveling to Saigon and Hanoi during the war.

He came out as a gay man in 1969, the year of the Stonewall Rebellion in the Village. "I never expected such a sea change on this issue," but he himself was a part of it.

A longtime resident of the East Village, he retired from the League in 1999 but by no means from activism. He has been the Socialist Party's co-chair twice and its standard-bearer for President of the United States in 1980 and 2000 as well as the Green Party's nominee for U.S. Senate in 2004. He has been arrested numerous times in demonstrations for civil rights, peace and worker's rights, including in 2005 to protest the Iraq War.

Sylvia Miles

ACTRESS

Twice nominated for an Academy Award—in 1970 for *Midnight Cowboy* and 1976 for *Farewell, My Lovely*, co-starring with Robert Mitchum—Sylvia Miles is still a force of nature! Raised in Greenwich Village, she made her stage debut in *A Stone for Danny Fisher* in 1956 and shortly followed with *The Iceman Cometh* at Circle in the Square as Margie in the legendary production with Jason Robards. Genet's *Balcony* followed two years later in the new Circle in the Square on Bleecker Street and *Night of the Iguana* at the uptown Circle in the Square in 1976-77 co-starring with Richard Chamberlain and Dorothy Maguire. Many plays and many films have followed including *Parrish*, Warhol's *Heat*, *Wall Street*, Agatha Christie's *Evil Under the Sun* starring opposite James Mason, *Crossing Delancey* and *She Devil*.

"I grew up in New York City. My dad had a furniture factory in Soho on Prince Street. While walking east on 14th Street each day to Washington Irving High School on 16th Street and Irving Place, I would daydream or imagine (fantasize was surely too extravagant a term for the street kid I was) that I was flat chested. It seemed indecent to be a 36C going on D at twelve years of age. I would then stop at Child's restaurant on 14th Street and University Place next to the old Orbach's and order tea and crumpets. The waitresses there—who were usually middle-aged, Irish, and not quite up to the higher class Schrafft's standard—would humor me by not mentioning that the 'crumpets' were really your packaged American English muffins.

"Oh, how elegant it was—I now felt flat chested, respectable, English, and very ladylike. After this daily pit stop at Child's, I would cut through Klein's department store and on to school. How vulgar! All the women in Klein's had big busts like me. When would I graduate to Bonwit Teller or Best & Co.? (Very flat-chested clothes in those stores, I was sure of that. Hadn't I seen them in the Sunday *Times* ads?)

"Many years later, in 1978, while sitting in a tea shop on Picadilly circus in London, staring at my name in lights as the star of Tennessee Williams's *Vieux Carré*, I sipped my tea, munched my real English crumpets, and mused on the irony of my early fantasy—for surely with all my dedication, diligence, determination, and utter tenacity, would I ever really made it without my 36C going on D?"

Rev. Howard Moody

PASTOR, JUDSON CHURCH

The Rev. Howard Moody, the pastor of the Judson Memorial Church on Washington Square Park for decades, remembers that "the new age of the '60s opened with a 'bang' that reverberated around the front door of Judson. The 'shot' was fired by a most unlikely troublemaker, the new Parks Commissioner, Newbold Morris. He enforced a ban on 'guitar-playing folksingers' in the park. On the first Sunday of the ban, folksingers and their friends marched peacefully into the park and, after the crowd had gathered around the fountain, the police decided to move them out. It resulted in a full-scale riot with many people injured by the police. Judson opened its doors to sign up the victims and there began a five-week protest that ended in Mayor Wagner rescinding the order. Singers sang again in our wonderful park."

Now Minister Emeritus, Rev. Moody continued an open door tradition for all of society's oppressed and outcast that remains to this day.

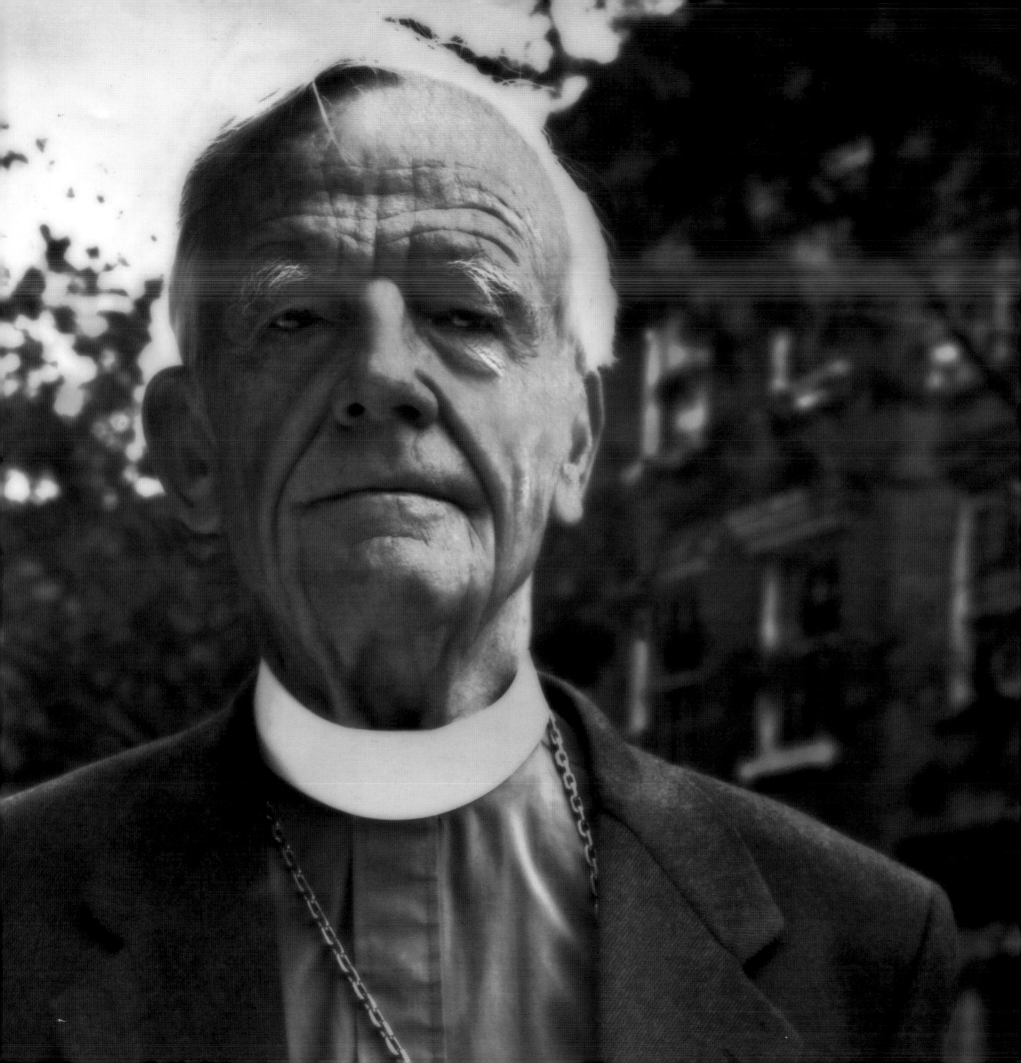

Rt. Rev. Paul Moore

EPISCOPAL BISHOP OF NEW YORK

The Rt. Rev. Paul Moore comes from the Moore family that owned the land from which Chelsea was developed, but after his stint as Episcopal Bishop of New York from 1972 to '89 up at the Cathedral of St. John the Divine, he retired to Greenwich Village, still staying active in social justice causes especially the plight of the people in East Timor.

"We live on the corner of Bank and West 4th Street," he told us in 1998. "One night, my wife Brenda was dozing in front of the TV. She awoke with a start to see a man shot down in cold blood on our corner. After a moment of shock, she realized that the scene was on the TV and not on the street. So much for life in the outdoor movie studio in the Village!"

Bishop Moore wrote several books including his memoirs *Take a Bishop Like Me* (1979) and *Presences: A Bishop's Life in the City* (1997). He died on May 1, 2003, at his home in the Village.

Robin Morgan

WRITER

An award-winning poet, novelist, political theorist, journalist and editor, Robin Morgan has published 18 books and been a leader of the international Women's Movement for 25 years. Recent books include *Upstairs in the Garden: Poems Selected and New*, *A Hot January: Poems 1996-1999*, *Saturday's Child: A Memoir*, *The Mer Child: A New Legend for Children and Other Adults*, and her acclaimed nonfiction work *The Demon Lover: The Roots of Terrorism*. She has traveled—as organizer, lecturer, and journalist—to all five continents, spending months in the Middle East's Palestinian refugee camps, yet always returns to Greenwich Village, where she has lived since 1983, to write and tend her city garden.

from her *Creation Myth*

Sightseers assume the great boulders in Central Park
are clever landscaping. . . .
I know they are over four hundred million
years old, ribs from the spine of crystalline bedrock
running under the surface of Manhattan Island.

. . . Each edge
becomes part of the middle, requiring a further edge.
Today I walk the Great Road, as it was called

once—now Greenwich Avenue, then the vast highway
cleared by the Iroquois, stretching north into Canada
—and chant my songs with the other ghostly runners
who shimmer through leafgreen-dappled time. Each center
becomes part of the rim, requiring a deeper core.

Let there be words for the naming of just such a moment,
when I round the corner into this quiet street
where small calley pear trees have exclaimed their bloom sudden
as a white spring mist overarching the path to my building:
And the evening and the morning are the first day.

Bruce Morrow

PHOTOGRAPHER, BROADCASTER, HUMANITARIAN

Perhaps all Americans don't see each other quite as brothers and sisters, but we are at least all cousins, related through veteran radio broadcaster Bruce Morrow—our "Cousin Brucie"—who has been binding us together through rock and roll and thick and thin since 1959. His is one of the most recognizable voices on the airwaves. Author of the best-selling book, *My Life and Rock and Roll,* Morrow is in the Radio Hall of Fame, Broadcasting and Cable's Hall of Fame and the National Association of Broadcasters Hall of Fame. Cousin Brucie is still going strong on Sirius satellite radio.

His far-flung fame notwithstanding, at the Village at Ennio & Michael Ristorante on LaGuardia Place, one of his neighborhood haunts, he talks about his photo exhibit on the walls, reflecting a passion for photography that he developed at the age of nine in Brooklyn. It is a stunning collection

Morrow founded WCAG radio station (now MNYU) at New York University, but got his start as a performer in a hygiene play at James Madison High School in Brooklyn. "Something awoke in me and I haven't stopped talking since," he said. "You have longevity in this business by being positive and warm not resorting to shocking people." He calls radio "our most intimate form of mass media" and considers the platform he has "an awesome responsibility."

He is deeply involved in raising money for good causes—often auctioning his own photographic works—especially for Variety: The Children's Charity, where he has served as president for a decade. There is a Cousin Brucie Asthma Center for Children at Montefiore in the Bronx.

His wife of more than 30 years, Jodie Berlin Morrow, with whom he has lived in the Village for more than 20 years, works with children with facial differences, using theater and communications, and works as a life coach.

Joan Nestle

WRITER AND HISTORIAN

Co-founder of the Lesbian Herstory Archives in 1973, Joan Nestle describes herself as "a 62-year old fem lesbian who came out in the working class bars of Greenwich Village in the late 1950s." The experience of these years and of the succeeding decades are told in *A Restricted Country, A Fragile Union* (Cleis Press, 1998) and *Persistent Desire: A Fem-Butch Reader* (Alyson Books, 1992). With John Preston, she co-edited *Sister and Brother: Lesbians and Gay Men Talk About Their Lives Together* and with Naomi Holoch she co-edited three volumes of *Women on Women*, collections of lesbian short fiction and *The Vintage Book of International Lesbian Fiction*. Her latest collection is *GenderQueer: Voices from Beyond the Binary*, edited with Riki Wilchins and Clare Howell. For 29 wonderful years, she was a teacher of writing in the SEEK Program at Queens College.

From her "Stone Butch, Drag Butch, Baby Butch," (originally in *A Restricted Country*, Firebrand Books, 1987; Cleis Books, 2003):

A hot dark night on Eighth Street.
Held tight with love,
the butch yells up to a shadow on the wall
all she can see of her lady
who calls out
"I'm here baby"
and we all hear her.
A shrine for separated lovers,
the Women's House of D.*
They tore it down
replaced it with a garden
but those voices still are there
the lasting blossoms of our surviving time.

Stone butch, drag butch, baby butch
I keep you deep within me
warning voices in a changing time:
Shame is the first betrayer.

*The Women's House of Detention stood for many years on the corner of Eight Street and Sixth Avenue in Greenwich Village. In the 1960s, I passed it every time I made my way to the Sea Colony bar across from Abingdon Square.

Jack Newfield

Veteran scribe Jack Newfield said that he had lived in the Village "almost forever," residing on West 8th, Morton and then Charlton Street. He was a legend at the *Village Voice* from 1964 to 1988 and continued his championing of forgotten people as a columnist for the *New York Post* before moving on to *The Nation*.

Newfield loved the diversity of the people in the Village, the many bookstores, and the creative artists. But politics was his beat.

"In late 1967," he said, "Pete Hammill and I brought Robert Kennedy into the Lion's Head to convince him to run for President because the Vietnam War was taking so much money away from cities and the War on Poverty. But the two bartenders were flustered to see Kennedy walk in because there was a pornographic graffiti in the men's room relating to Jackie Kennedy. They kept giving us frantic messages not to let Bobby use the men's room to give them time to paint over it or wash it off. It was the high and low of politics going on in the Lion's Head."

Jack Newfield died on December 20, 2004, at the age of 66.

Sister Marita Rose O'Brien

NURSE AND VILLAGE NATIVE

A nurse at St. Vincent's Hospital, Sister Marita Rose O'Brien was "born in the same house on West 12th Street that my family still has" she said at the time she was interviewed. They subsequently sold it because the nine children in her family had all moved out.

"I left home in '44 to enter the convent and go to nursing school at St. Vincent's," she said.

Sister O'Brien remembered a Village of her childhood that "was homier and closer" than the one many still enjoy today. Families occupied whole houses. "We played stoop ball on our stoop in the summer and used to sleigh ride down a hill on West 4th Street in winter going from Bank to West 12th. We played King of the Mountain on the piled-up snow."

In later years, "I had a brother who was a priest cleaning the snow and chopping the ice on our sidewalk on West 12th. Without looking up, he saw someone's feet walk up to him. 'Oh hello, Mrs. Congress Lady,' he said. And Bella Abzug said, 'Hello, Mr. Priest,' even though he wasn't wearing anything to indicate that he was. Everyone knew everyone else."

Odetta

SINGER

Odetta is renowned as the first major influence on such legends in their own right as Joan Baez, Bob Dylan, Janis Joplin, Judy Collins, Sweet Honey in the Rock, Tracy Chapman, Cassandra Wilson and Jewel, among countless others.

She has taken her guitar and passionate folk singing—not to mention blues, spirituals, jazz, and movement songs—around the nation and throughout the world. But the Village has always been a special place for performing and listening to great music for her.

Sitting in the Bitter End on Bleecker Street, she said, "I remember in the '60s when we would be on the road for three months at a time, I'd get home, put my suitcase and Baby—that's my guitar—down and head to the Village to one of the clubs and hear folksingers and go home as happy as a lark. It was like food or being refilled at the gas station." One time she had to be at NBC for the "Today" show at 5 a.m., so she just "stayed up with the kids" in a Village club all night.

"The Village allowed painters and writers and music to happen," she said. "It wouldn't happen on 86th Street." She has been recording for more than 50 years, and her 2003 album, *Lookin' for a Home*, is a tribute to the music and life of Leadbelly.

After September 11, 2001, the usually irreverent David Letterman wanted to lend some dignity to its return to the air. Dave did it by opening with Odetta, singing a medley of *We Shall Overcome* and *This Little Light of Mine* and closing with her rendition of another of her standards, *Amazing Grace*.

Jay Oliva

UNIVERSITY PRESIDENT

Former New York University President Jay Oliva said, "I never walk the streets of the Village without remembering my immigrant grandparents, immigrants from Genoa, who came to Carmine Street toward the end of the last century. They were married in Our Lady of Pompeii. I remember my grandfather vividly. He was one tough character who was never content with anything. If I were to say, 'Grandpa, I've just become president of New York University,' he would say, 'Well, then, don't mess it up!' If one accepted that kind of responsibility, then one was expected to do it in a fashion to bring honor to the family. I have always kept that clearly in mind. And I keep in mind each day in the Village the struggles that were part of beginning lives in a new country."

Philip Pavia

SCULPTOR

Philip Pavia is not just a great sculptor, but a forceful organizer in the art world who founded The Club in Greenwich Village for his fellow artists and dubbed the work they were crafting "Abstract Expressionism."

The Whitney Museum was on 8th Street in those early days, and Pavia lamented that the Village is "pricing out artists." He remembered during the war when Washington Square Park was "the center for refugees, writers, and artists" and the Waldorf Cafeteria on Sixth Avenue and 8th Street was their haven for coffee and arguing. They established The Club in 1948 at 39 East 8th St.

Early members included Jackson Pollack, Willem de Kooning, and Leo Castelli. "It was a tidal change" in the art world, he said, and the writer John O'Hara "was always trying to take over. Everyone lived within two or three blocks of it." Kay Larson wrote in *The Times* that The Club "was home to a rampantly individualistic generation of irascibles who thought ideas were worth fighting for, and who brandished egos like closed fists." They would repair to the Cedar Tavern on University Place after their meetings.

When Pavia and his fellow artists gathered in East Hampton, long before it was fashionable and pricey, they played baseball. "Jackson didn't play with us," he said, "he thought we were terrible. Nice guy. Sad story." Pollock died in a car crash there in 1956.

Critic Phyllis Braff once wrote of Pavia that he "builds on the sense of touch inherent in carved marble." Pavia's work is now in collections around the world from Paris to Pietrasanta, Italy, and in New York's own Whitney Museum and the Metropolitan Museum of Art. The lobby of the Hippodrome building on West 43rd Street Exhibits his *Ides of March*.

Philip Pavia died on April 13, 2005, at 94.

Estelle Parsons

ACTRESS AND DIRECTOR

"I always wanted to be a Greenwich Village person," said Estelle Parsons, "but I was never part of the downtown crowd. I'm more Middle American."

Parsons did have a house at 16 W. 12th St. when she first married and another at W. 11th off Sixth Avenue when she had twins. "We went to Washington Square Park where the playground is," she said. The Village "is more like home if you're from out of town," said Parsons, who hails from Marblehead, Massachusetts. "I made my best friends down there," she said, including artist and activist Roz Roose.

Parsons eventually moved to the Upper West Side "because it was cheaper," getting a six-room apartment for $165 a month.

With a background in law, she got her start in New York as a writer, producer, and commentator for NBC's *Today* show in the days of Dave Garroway and J. Fred Muggs.

Her first play was at the Cherry Lane Theatre and she worked another playhouse, now gone, on Bleecker Street "where Lenny Bruce was performing in the basement." At the Theatre de Lys on Christopher Street, now the Lucille Lortel, she wore a suit of armor in Arthur Kopit's *Asylum* and did *The Threepenny Opera*. She had a longtime association with Joseph Papp, who was headquartered at the East Village landmark Public Theatre. She has received four Tony nominations for her work on Broadway, including a tour-de-force in *Miss Margarida's Way* in 1978. She has directed productions of *Macbeth*, *As You Like It* and *Romeo and Juliet* as well as Oscar Wilde's *Salome* starring Al Pacino in 2003.

In her long and continuing film career, she won an Academy Award for Best Supporting Actress in *Bonnie and Clyde* in 1967 and was nominated the following year for *Rachel, Rachel*. She gained a whole new audience playing Roseanne's mother Beverly in the TV series *Roseanne*.

In 2005, Estelle Parsons was inducted into the Theatre Hall of Fame and received an Honorary Degree of Fine Arts from Connecticut College.

Lawrence J. Quirk

FILM HISTORIAN

Lawrence J. Quirk has authored more than thirty books and is considered by some to be the ultimate film historian. His vast knowledge and research of American film has led to bios of some of Hollywood's most famous, including Joan Crawford, Bob Hope, Ingrid Bergman, Warren Beatty, Lauren Bacall, Katharine Hepburn and James Stewart. And, among his favorites, The Rat Pack.

He's lived on Charles Street since the late 1950s and has bittersweet memories of his early days in the Village.

"I fell in love with a young actor, now famous, who shall remain nameless. We were involved for two years. He lived on Perry Street in a floor-through apartment and his rent was $60. I still find myself going by that sad little tenement about twice a week and standing outside for a moment. We had the kind of love that I thought would go on forever."

Lynn Redgrave

ACTRESS AND PLAYWRIGHT

Lynn Redgrave has graced stages and screens, large and small, for decades of outstanding work, from her breakout performance as *Georgy Girl* in 1966 to James Whales' housekeeper in *Gods and Monsters* in 1999, winning Golden Globes and garnering Oscar nominations for both. She wrote *Shakespeare for My Father*, integrating Shakespearian scenes with memories of her actor father, Sir Michael Redgrave, and performed it around the world, including on Broadway. And in just a few minutes in the film *Kinsey* as one of his study subjects, she masterfully provided the emotional climax of the film by conveying what the doctor's work meant to her as the once-isolated lesbian she portrayed.

Redgrave was a founder of the Royal National Theatre in London, working with such legends as her father, Laurence Olivier, Noel Coward, Maggie Smith and Tom Courtenay. She has thrice been nominated for the Tony Award, including in 2006 for *The Constant Wife*. And she won the Drama Desk Award for best featured actress for her unforgettable turn in *Miss Fozzard Finds Her Feet*, one of the monologues from Alan Bennett's *Talking Heads* at the Minetta Lane Theatre in the Village in 2003, the same year her sister Vanessa won best actress for *Long Day's Journey into Night*.

It is 2003 that Lynn Redgrave recalled while sitting for her portrait in the Minetta Lane. "This was a very special place to me," she said. "It doesn't have a good dressing room. Just a little box—a little haven."

The Minetta Lane and the Village were her refuge that year while she battled breast cancer and cared for her dying mother, Rachel Kempson, Lady Redgrave. "I came down to the Village on the F train, with those end-less steps at West Fourth Street that got harder as my chemo went on. But I'd go to the falafel place on Macdougal Street and stay at a friend's place on Sullivan on a double show day. My friend, Ann, would leave me little goodies. Coming here was like a sanctuary."

Redgrave said, "At the end of the show, I would feel so good I'd go to the Minetta Tavern for a glass of wine. I never lived in the Village, but wish I had." During that time, she said, "a big chunk of my day was sleeping to be able to come here" and perform. "I look at it as one of the happiest times in my theatre life."

She loves Village audiences. "They usually really want to see the play," she said, "because people who aren't as dedicated can't find their way to the Village."

Frank Riessman

PROFESSOR, EDITOR, AUTHOR

The Village Vanguard had a special place in the heart of Frank Riessman.

"We used to go to the jazz clubs regularly when I was young. The Vanguard on Seventh Avenue was a favorite spot. One night I went to hear Carmen McCrae sing and I swear she sang just to me that night. I was 19. She was 43. After the set, she talked with us at our table. I asked her for a date. She said she was too old for me."

Riessman was the founding editor of *Social Policy* magazine, a journal about social movements, and the author or editor of 16 books including *The Inner City Child* and *The Self-Help Revolution*.

He developed the "helper therapy principle" that holds that in helping relationships, the person giving the help receives even more benefit than the person being helped. In self-help groups, people with a particular problem such as alcoholism help maintain their own sobriety in Alcoholics Anonymous by helping newer members maintain their sobriety.

He died at age 79 on March 1, 2004.

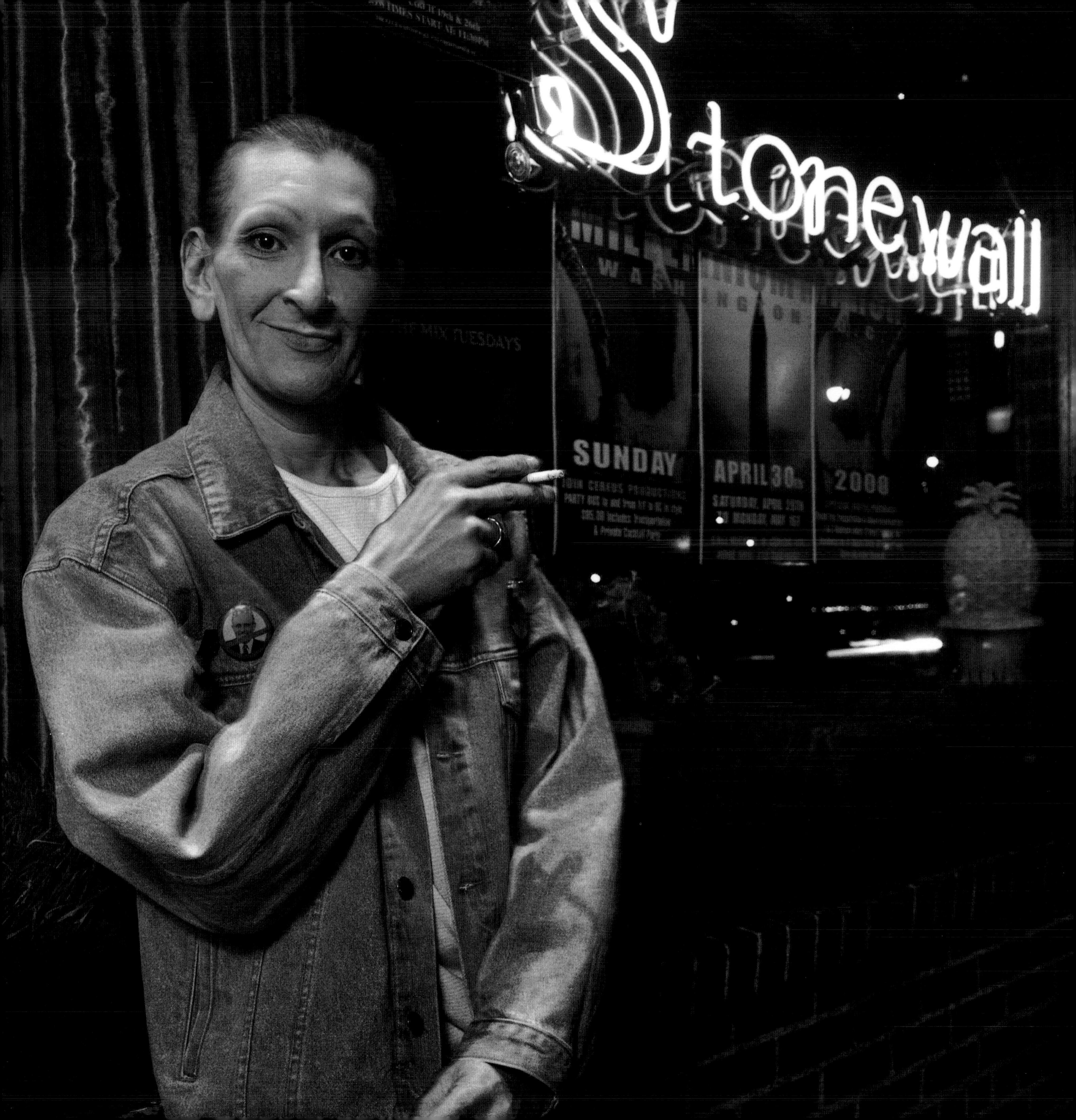
Stonewall
MIX TUESDAYS
SUNDAY
APRIL 30th
2000

Sylvia Rivera

TRANSGENDER ACTIVIST AND PIONEER

Sylvia Rivera was out on her own longer than most people decades older. Rivera left home on the Lower East Side at age 10, and just survived most all those years, many on the streets.

In 1969, Rivera was at the center of a turning point in world history that took place in Sheridan Square. Police had raided the Stonewall Inn and gay people fought back with unprecedented militancy. The police barricaded themselves inside the bar. The riots continued, with Rivera on the front lines of the battle, for three nights and neither the Village nor the gay, lesbian, bisexual, and transgendered communities have been the same since.

Rivera remembered the days when transgendered folk were "pushed under the rug" in the gay community, even as it fought for its own liberation. So in 1970, Rivera founded, with the late Marsha Johnson, Street Transvestites Action Revolutionaries (STAR), originally a cell of the Gay Liberation Front. "We were mostly transgendered kids and some butch lesbian women," said Rivera, who was active in her later years in the community's Transgender Council, bringing diverse groups together to develop a residence for transgendered youth.

Toward the end of her life, Rivera lived in "Tranny House" in Brooklyn with partner, Julia Murray, and worked at the Uplift lamp store on Hudson Street above Christopher, run by Randy Wicker, himself a Village legend and early gay activist.

Rivera died February 9, 2002, at the age of 50. The Metropolitan Community Church's shelter for homeless LGBT youth is named in her honor.

Rev. Herb Rogers, S.J.

PRIEST, PROFESSOR, ACTIVIST

The Rev. Herb Rogers lived as a boy in Chelsea, but moved to the 67 Perry Street in the Village in 1921 when their block had to make way for the massive London Terrace Apartments. Rogers became an altar boy at St. Joseph's, the oldest Catholic church in the City, where Mayor Jimmy Walker attended. He also served mass at the old women's prison (now a park next to the Jefferson Library) "where there were murderers and famous cases," he said.

At St. Francis Xavier High School on 16th Street, he refused to participate in military activities because "a Christian shouldn't carry a gun," he said, which was the beginning of his lifelong work for peace and justice. He entered the Jesuits in 1930, was ordained in 1944, and taught at various places before arriving at Fordham University in 1955 in the theology and philosophy departments. He befriended colorful artists along the way from Brendan Behan (whom he tried to sober up) to Paul Morrissey and Andy Warhol (who spoke to his class).

But growing up in the Village meant "everybody writing lived next door," from Willa Cather to e.e. cummings, who lived on Patchin Place, Rogers' favorite. He also remembers the Pirate's Den in Sheridan Square, "where the workers dressed like pirates for the tourists."

"My hobby was arguing and the great art was conversations that went on for days in Union Square. You'd go to sleep, come back, and resume the argument. Once we almost got arrested for disturbing the peace because the cops thought we were fighting."

Rogers died on March 3, 2007, at the age of 95.

Rollerena

NEW YORK'S FAIRY GODMOTHER

Rollerena, New York's Fairy Godmother, has been tooling around the Village and elsewhere in the City for decades, delighting all with exquisite roller skating, a magical gown, bestowing the touch of a healing baton that confers love and liberation on everyone. Here is the story, in Rollerena's own words:

"I went from a Bluegrass Belle of three counties in my native Kentucky to the Queen of Studio 54. What started out as an alternate means of travel in May 1970 to a Midtown nine-to-five job blossomed into a full-fledged career of roller skating.

"The Rollerena character was 'born' on Saturday, September 16, 1972, on Christopher Street at The Opulent Era (now closed). I enjoyed the people I met around the City and the Gay Pride parades. To this day, I exchange many fond memories and when old timers approach me, we reminisce about the Golden Era of the '70s.

"On October 14, 2003, the National Archive of Lesbian, Gay, Bisexual, and Transgender History honored me with an exhibit at the LGBT Community Center. I have donated my skates, gown, accessories and other memorabilia to the National Archives. The way I am now is the 're-born' Rollerena.

"I was in Vietnam during the Stonewall uprising [in 1969 in the Village] and after returning to Manhattan in the late '60s just eight months later, I put on those roller skates and I have been madly in love with the City ever since."

Rollerena is not just an institution in the gay community, but a reminder of the Village when it was full of creative characters in classes by themselves, enriching street life immeasurably.

Ned Rorem

COMPOSER AND WRITER

Shortly after World War II, Ned Rorem moved to New York after Virgil Thomson asked him to be his copyist. He lived on $20 a week, with $5 going for rent to Morris Golde with whom he had fallen in love. They lived at 123 West 11th St."All my friends lived nearby," he said. "but in '49, I went to visit Europe and didn't come back." He did take the notes that would eventually become his notorious *Paris Diary*, and compose the world's greatest art songs.

Rorem returned to the Village and W. 12th Street in 1957, living above the Beatrice Inn. Bill Flanagan "was my best friend—he was living with Edward Albee. We went to the Old Colony, the 8th Street Bar and Julius'. The Village was the center of the universe." He remembers Drossie's restaurant on Greenwich Avenue run by Russian sisters—"a gay-centered bohemian place with great Russian food. And if we couldn't pay, they let us pay the next time."

His parents moved to New York in 1964 and settled on Charles Street "until they went off to a retirement home," he said. "I met Jim Holmes the year after and we moved to West 70th Street," where Ned remains alone today, Jim having died in 1999.

"The Village is always a frame of mind. But art needs tension and young artists go to Hoboken now," he said with the finality that marks many of the pronouncements in his diaries.

"When I go to the Village now, I look around at all the places where I lost my virginity," he said. "For me, Paris is full of dead people I know who were a generation older. The Village is full of post-adolescent élan."

David Rothenberg

David Rothenberg, a theatrical publicist and Village resident since 1964, has served his community as a gay activist, candidate for City Council and host of his own radio show on WBAI. But his long stint as executive director of The Fortune Society for ex-offenders had its roots in a play that he produced in 1967 at the Actor's Playhouse in the Village about prison life called *Fortune and Men's Eyes*. At a discussion with the audience after one show "someone said that it was exaggeration," Rothenberg recalls. "A guy in the back said, 'Not if my 20 years in prison counted for anything. When the lights came on, I thought I was back in jail.' He joined us on stage. He said if he came back he'd bring a black ex-con because there was white time and black time. We started having groupies at the weekly dialogues—ex-cons, relatives of inmates. They'd read about it in *The Times*: 'The Drama Continues after the Curtain Falls.' We realized that audiences were fascinated and ignorant of what happens in prison. Nobody who did time came out about it. They were hiding their pasts. We wanted to educate the public about conditions in prison so we founded The Fortune Society. When Attica happened, we had people in place. It made a big difference."

Rothenberg said "there's no place I'd rather live" than the Village. "In the '60s especially, there was a sense of freedom compared to the rest of America. And it was where Paul Robeson could perform in the '20s."

Florence Rush

AUTHOR AND FEMINIST ACTIVIST

Florence Rush was born in Manhattan, grew up in the Bronx, spent much of her adult life in the suburbs and moved to Greenwich Village in 1974 at the age of 56 to be "where the action is." She was already involved in groups such as NY Radical Feminists and Women's Strike for Peace and would later help to organize Older Women's Liberation.

It was at a Radical Feminists conference held at Washington Irving HS that Rush, a psychiatric social worker, did a presentation on the abuse of children. "I was the first to offer a feminist perspective," she said and it led to her breakthrough book in 1980, *Sexual Abuse of Children: A Feminist Point of View*. She subsequently became one of the most widely quoted and sought after experts on the subject in the country.

When her son, Matthew, told her in 1987 that he had AIDS, "I dropped everything and became an AIDS activist." Through the People with AIDS Coalition (PWAC), she got involved with a support group for mothers that met in a little apartment off the garden of St. John's Episcopal Church. Her son died in June 1990, six weeks after his partner, Ron. Rush had cared for both of them. Because Ron's fundamentalist parents blamed their son for his condition, Rush wrote a searing "Open Letter to the Parents of My Son's Lover" in the PWAC Newsline: "I don't regret one moment of my involvement, but it was you he wanted and your rejection of him was almost as painful as his illness." Rush moved on to the Mother's Bereavement Group that once met at the Village Nursing Home.

She is still active in feminist causes, mostly in the Village. "My friends say that if I go above 14th Street, I get the bends."

Susan Sarandon

ACTOR AND ACTIVIST

Though born in Manhattan, Susan Sarandon was raised in the suburbs and first experienced downtown through the East Village clubs she frequented when she returned to live in Manhattan. "It seemed so exotic in the '70s," she said. "Now I'm completely at home here." After working her way down a series of West Side apartments in adult life, she got to University and 9th before bumping back up into Chelsea. Her partner, Tim Robbins, grew up in the Village and her children have all gone to school downtown.

"I love the scale of the Village. It's so European," said Sarandon who has lived in Italy. "As an observer of people, the Village is the place to be. You just couldn't create intentionally what happens here spontaneously— the way you're always running into people and constantly coming upon things that you didn't plan or schedule in your life." She is also thrilled to have been able to raise her children here, where "they become independent so much sooner than in the suburbs, learning to get around on their own, seeing so many different kinds of people."

Playing artist Alice Neel in the movie *Joe Gould's Secret*, set in the Greenwich Village of the 1950s, Sarandon said, "I got real insight into the Village as a village, when it was dominated by artists and they all knew each other and looked out for one another."

Sarandon is involved in a myriad of causes that are in or touch the Village from Housing Works to the Hetrick-Martin Institute to Village Care of New York.

John Sebastian

SINGER AND SONGWRITER

Mark Sebastian

SINGER, SONGWRITER, REAL ESTATE BROKER

The Sebastian brothers grew up at 29 Washington Square West, down the hall from Eleanor Roosevelt. They are the children of John, a harmonica virtuoso, and Jane, a radio writer who later managed Carnegie Hall.

As a boy, Mark played a unique game under the Washington Square Arch, whacking a pink ball off its curves. Mark jokes that some of his Spaldines are still lodged in the rosettes of the masonry.

Older brother John remembers the real Village legends who roamed the park, including Big Black, "an ex-prize fighter who walked around with the air of an African king," and "a wonderful gay man from the West Village who wore medieval costume and looked like a character out of Don Quixote." He counted them as friends.

As a teen, Mark wrote *Summer in the City*. John rewrote the verse and it became the first hit for his group, The Lovin' Spoonful. It is an anthem of New York life that continues to resonate today.

John's musical life began as an amateur in Washington Square. Soon he had jobs accompanying Fred Neil and Tim Hardin at the Playhouse Café during its period as a coffeehouse. From there he graduated to accompanist/roadie for John Hurt at the Gaslight. After a solo stint at Charlie Washburn's Third Side, he met Zal Yanovsky and began playing at the Night Owl Café, the Café Bizarre, and rehearsing in the basement of the Albert Hotel, now a co-op on West 10th Street, preparing The Lovin' Spoonful with songs like *Do You Believe in Magic* and *Daydream*. In 1969, he soloed at Woodstock.

John has enjoyed a long and continuing solo career after the Spoonful.

Mark, who played the Gaslight and Café au Go Go as a youth, pursued songwriting and acting in California, including collaborations with Brian Wilson of the Beach Boys and helping establish LaMama West, the West Coast satellite of the legendary East Village theatre. He wrote the #1 hit *Stutter* by Joe that won ASCAP's 2001 Rhythm & Soul Award and a BMI 2002 Urban Award. In addition to producing independent films, he is a real estate broker with Douglas Elliman right in the heart of the Village.

Marian Seldes

ACTOR AND TEACHER

Marian Seldes has been gracing the New York stage from the Village to Broadway for decades now. She made her stage debut in *Medea* in 1947 and won the 1967 Tony Award for Featured Actress in Edward Albee's *A Delicate Balance*, the beginning of a lifetime of interpreting his work including *Three Tall Women* and *The Play about the Baby*. Four more Tony nominations followed, as did a record for longevity—appearing in *Deathtrap* from 1978 through 1982 without missing a performance. She was inducted into the Theatre Hall of Fame in 1996.

Seldes studied acting at the Neighborhood Playhouse under Sanford Meisner and had a distinguished career at the Juilliard School for 24 years, teaching such students as Kevin Kline, Patti Lupone, Kevin Spacey, Christopher Reeve and Laura Linney. "When you're teaching acting," she said, "there's no one in the room who does not want to learn. It's like an aphrodisiac. You don't want to go home."

The daughter of journalist Gilbert Seldes and niece of journalist George Seldes, Marian has written an acclaimed memoir, *The Bright Lights: A Theatre Life*, and a novel, *Time Together*. And she has brought a touch of class to many movies and television shows, including HBO's *If These Walls Could Talk 2* as Vanessa Redgrave's lifetime partner and *Truman*, where she played Eleanor Roosevelt.

Seldes said, "I've always had a love affair with Greenwich Village. My life as a New Yorker has been enriched by the poets, painters, playwrights, novelists and choreographers who lived in the Village. The plays I have seen and the theatres I have played there changed my life. The history of the modern theatre in America— from Eugene O'Neill to Edward Albee—at the Provincetown Playhouse is legendary."

The Village, she said, "has been and is today a haven for all creative artists. It is a place of opportunities, of possibilities." She loves "the shape of the streets, the size of the buildings, the visible sky, the humanness."

"It is the most embraceable part of our city," she said.

Dr. Joseph Sonnabend

PIONEERING AIDS PHYSICIAN

The Village welcomes immigrants from all over the country and world, including Dr. Joseph Sonnabend from South Africa by way of England who moved to it in 1967. But as one of the first doctors to see in 1979 what would eventually come to be known as AIDS, he put the vaunted tolerance of the Village to the test. In 1985, the co-op board of the West 12th Street building that housed his office tried not to renew his lease. The board president "was quite happy to tell me that people with AIDS were going through the building and people who had just purchased their apartments were worried about property values dropping," he said.

"A sympathetic person made a recording" of that statement and Sonnabend, with the help of Lambda Legal Defense, was able to win the first AIDS civil rights case in the city's history. He also had "wonderful letters of support from other people in the building."

Sonnabend went on to co-found the American Foundation for AIDS Research, but remembers the early days of the AIDS crisis as a time when too few people—especially doctors who were treating cases—spoke out about the deadly new syndrome that they were seeing. "They wanted the glory. It was a selfish period. There was an amazing non-response."

Frances Sternhagen

ACTRESS

Frances Sternhagen was an accomplished actress in her native Washington, D.C. before coming to the Village in the 1950s. She played in *Thieves' Carnival* at the Cherry Lane Theatre in 1956, and lived with three friends at 75½ Bedford St., the narrowest house in the city, where Edna St. Vincent Millay dwelled in 1923 and 1924. "My friend from Vassar leased it, and we had to pay what seemed like a lot of money–$70 a month each."

Sternhagen won an Obie and the Clarence Derwent Award for *The Admirable Bashville* at the Cherry Lane in '56. She did *The Red Eye of Love* and *The Pinter Plays* at the Provincetown Playhouse (a second Obie) and Shaw's *Misalliance* at the Sheridan Square Playhouse. While doing Beckett's *Play* at the Cherry Lane under the direction of the great Alan Schneider, she was ensconced in an urn. She said, "I was pregnant, so the urn solved the costume problem."

Since her Village days, Sternhagen has proven herself one of the great actors of our time. On Broadway, she's had six Tony nominations and won it twice, for *The Good Doctor* and *The Heiress*. Off Broadway, besides those previously mentioned, she's appeared in *Driving Miss Daisy*, *A Perfect Ganesh* and *The Exact Center of the Universe*. Some of her film appearances include *The Hospital*, *Outland* and *Misery*, and TV audiences recognize her from *Cheers*, *ER*, *Law and Order* and *Sex and the City*. In 2003, she was at the Minetta Lane in Alan Bennett's affecting *Talking Heads*, which won Obies and an Outer Critics' Circle Award. She was happy to reconnect with the Village.

Ellen Stewart

MOTHER OF LA MAMA EXPERIMENTAL THEATER CLUBN

Since 1962 when she founded Café La Mama, Ellen Stewart has produced almost 2,000 plays written by a *Who's Who* of the theater—Shaw, Beckett, Ionesco, Gide, Pinter, Sam Shepard, Ed Bullins, van Itallie, Maria Irene Fornes, Adrienne Kennedy, Julie Bavasso, Gertrude Stein, Terrence McNally, Lanford Wilson, Charles Ludlam, Brecht, Robert Patrick, Warhol, and Shakespeare (in Korean) to name just a handful. Acting alumni include Nick Nolte, Billy Crystal, F. Murray Abraham, Robert De Niro, André De Shields, Estelle Getty, Al Pacino and Bette Midler. Tom O'Horgan, of *Hair* fame, was one of her founding directors. "Eighty percent of what is now considered the American theater originated at La MaMa," said Harvey Fierstein, another alumnus. And LaMama has been home to a host of international theater companies as well.

Stewart came to New York in 1950 to study design (having been barred in Illinois because of her race) and was successful at it, getting involved in theater when she rented an East 9th Street space in '61 for her brother and other playwrights to produce their work. So many men came to help fix up the space that neighbors complained it was a house of prostitution. The inspector who came to investigate was a former actor who helped her open it as a coffeehouse, theater licenses being hard to obtain.

"Ed Koch had me arrested on several occasions for doing entertainment without a license," Stewart recalled. "He was working with Commissioner Robert Moses to clean up the Village and I was the one he cleaned up. I had the honor of being in jail at the women's penitentiary right in the Village. Once I got to our present theater in the East Village, he pursued me, but I didn't have to go to jail. In the '80s, as mayor, he tried to foreclose for back taxes on our Great Jones Street rehearsal space, but he did not succeed. Later on, I was in City Hall being given a citation and he came up to me and said, 'How about a truce?' We shook hands and that was it."

About her work as a producer, she once wrote, "I'm not interested in the play. I'm interested in the person. If the person beeps, we do it. And if the play's a flop, I'm not bothered because I believe in that person." That faith is still going strong at 74-A E. 4th St. and throughout the world of theater that Ellen Stewart has touched.

Catharine Stimpson

PROFESSOR, NYU DEAN, WRITER

Growing up in Bellingham, Washington, Catharine Stimpson "always thought that New York was paradise" where people "went to the theatre, read books and the possibility of meeting a kindred soul was enhanced." Today, as university professor and dean of the Graduate School of Arts and Science at New York University, she surveys her dream of the Village from her massive office windows looking south over Washington Square.

The Village is the place that has been a nurturing home to Stimpson as she has become one of the country's leading educators and writers—she is director of the MacArthur Fellows Program, vice provost at Rutgers, director of the first Women's Center at Barnard and president of the Modern Language Association, among many other accomplishments.

Stimpson gets to live on Washington Square, too, but recalls living in the other New York in a loft on the Bowery starting in 1963 and long enough "to see crack replace alcohol" on the street. After being evicted, she moved to live with her partner, Elizabeth Wood, and four children on Seventh Avenue South, keeping an office in the meatpacking district. "We specialized in neighborhoods before they became fashionable," she said. "My identity is rooted in New York and what it represents," especially the Village's "myth of creativity and freedom and companionship. I don't mean to seem naïve. I know about the economic problems and gentrification, but thank God for historic preservation. The Village is like any other precious ecology—it always has to be fought for."

Sister Eileen Storey

PEACE ACTIVIST

Sister Eileen Storey lives in a community of the Sisters of Charity on Washington Square—when she is not dwelling in the Iraqi desert as a "witness for peace" or walking the streets of Baghdad as an American presence as she was when U.S. bombs were dropping there in 1991. She has also been the chaplain at Marymount Manhattan College and is the author of *Building the City of God* and *American – Salaam – Iraq*.

"The Village hides many pockets of high energy," she said. "We're one—those of us who gather on Monday nights to meditate for the City. As a Sister of Charity of New York, I'm at home here, just being a sister to those who walk the streets of the Village: the successful and the disadvantaged, the young and the old, the joggers and the shufflers.

"When I bring supplies to Iraq, doctors and children respond warmly to my 'I'm from New York.' They think that, like them, I'm a survivor. And I am. Saved from mediocrity by the heartbeat of Greenwich Village and the dynamism of New York City."

Roy Strickland
FLORIST AND GAY ACTIVIST

William Wynkoop
ENGLISH PROFESSOR AND GAY ACTIVIST

In their later years, Roy Strickland and William Wynkoop smashed stereotypes by being themselves—an older gay couple, appearing on shows such as *Phil Donahue*. They had become active in SAGE when it first started in the 1970s and became friendly visitors.

But their love story began on a park bench in Washington Square Park "one very mild December evening in 1948," Roy recalled. "William came along and saw me sitting there and he sat on the other end of the bench. We started talking and seemed to like each other. We went to a bar on 8th Street and had two beers. Then I said, 'Would you like to come back to my apartment and I'll give you another beer there?'" And so their relationship was born in a brownstone on West 12th Street. They dated on weekends for a while, alternating at each other's place.

Their relationship survived the difficulties of the pre-gay liberation era and William's taking a job at Wayne State in Detroit. Through a friend, Roy got a job in relatively nearby Cleveland at Bonwit Teller as display manager and they maintained their connection. But after a year and half, they both missed the city. William then landed a job at a college near New York and Roy joined a florist company in Manhattan, eventually getting his own shop that served the likes of the Vanderbilts, Whitneys and Paleys.

"We loved the Village," Roy said. "We felt at home there."

Roy Strickland and William Wynkoop were pioneers in the movement for equal marriage rights for gay couples, tying the knot at a public demonstration in 1996. William died at 87 on May 24, 2003, and Roy at 85 just two months later on July 28.

Jerry Tallmer

JOURNALIST

Manhattan-born Jerry Tallmer started hanging in the Village as a Dartmouth College undergraduate editor, an Air Force T/Sgt on short leaves and a discharged World War II GI. His first postwar Village address was 246 West 10th St.; next, a brownstone at 62 Perry St. owned by three maiden ladies—an anthropologist, a Viking editor, and a theater manager—and it was at one of their parties, lorded over by a cane-thumping Margaret Mead, that Tallmer got talking with fellow WW II vet Edwin C. Fancher, a large red-bearded psychologist and furniture mover who wanted to have all of Greenwich Village declared a landmark.

The countercultural *Village Voice* was founded in 1955 by four ex-enlisted men, publisher Fancher, editor Daniel Wolf, investor/columnist Norman Mailer, and Tallmer as "back of the book" editor of theater, movies, the arts. Each of the four had a different concept for the paper, a journal at any rate, more reflective of the creative juices of the Village than the then long-established, fuddy-duddy *The Villager,* which today, more than half-a-century later, is itself a very different and more vital newspaper itself.

In the first years of the *Voice* nobody (except the secretaries) was paid anything, but Tallmer got to write appreciations of dramatists from Chekhov to Beckett to Genet to Lorraine Hansberry to Irene Fornes to points north and south. He created and ran the Off-Broadway Obie Awards from 1956 to 1962, and somewhere in that stretch followed Harold Clurman as recipient of the George Jean Nathan Award in Drama Criticism.

It was the legendary Murray Kempton who suggested that Dorothy Schiff's liberal daily, *The New York Post,* bring this new talent onto staff, and it was for that newspaper that, starting in 1962, Tallmer would write thousands of pieces as a reporter, profiler, drama critic, film critic, art columnist, feature writer and occasional TV critic, as well as editing other thousands by other writers. Thirty-two years later, Rupert Murdoch broke the union (the local Newspaper Guild) and laid off 287 human beings—one of them Jerry Tallmer.

He shortly afterward got a call from Tom Butson, late great editor of the reborn *Villager.* Since 1994, Tallmer has been writing for that paper and its two associated weeklies, *Downtown Express* and the *Gay City News,* and the monthly magazine *Thrive,* gracing its pages with profiles ranging from Jules Feiffer to Pete Hamill to Ben Gazzara to Elaine Stritch to Mario Cuomo.

Calvin Trillin

WRITER, HUMORIST, COMPOSER OF DOGGEREL

Calvin Trillin is a longtime resident of the Village and has often drawn attention in his work to its hidden treasures such as the Pink Tea Cup restaurant.

He shared this story: "In the early days of the Village Halloween Parade, an intensely political character I used to refer to in columns as Harold the Communist wanted our younger daughter to go as Emma Goldman. She went as a box of M&M's instead. He thought our older daughter should go as 'The Dangers Posed to Our Society by the Military Industrial Complex.' I said, 'Harold, we don't have anybody at home who can sew that well.' She eventually decided to go that year as a chocolate chip ice-cream cone with chocolate sprinkles."

George Weinberg

PSYCHOLOGIST AND AUTHOR

George Weinberg is a clinical psychologist and psychotherapist in New York City who takes a dim view of many in his profession, and he is a heterosexual—none would call him "straight"—who has done more to advance the cause of gay liberation than anyone of his sexual orientation.

In 1972, Weinberg wrote, *Society and the Healthy Homosexual*, coining the term "homophobia" for the irrational fear of and hatred against gay people at a time when the American Psychiatric Association still classified homosexuality as a mental illness. "My book rallied a lot of gay people to join gay groups and fight for gay rights," he said, coming as it did just three years after the Stonewall Rebellion in the Village that sparked the modern gay rights movement. By 1973, the APA had voted overwhelmingly to remove homosexuality from its index of mental disorders.

Although he moved to the Upper West Side 30 years ago, Weinberg has Village roots, having taken his masters in English at New York University—though he advised, "If you really love something, don't take it in school." Years later he would renew his love for the Bard of Avon in *Shakespeare on Love*, one of his thirteen books.

"The Village meant heterogeneity, anonymity and getting away from home and family," he said. "It was electrical. You could walk through its parks, talk to anyone, be with anyone, and appear any way you wanted with no one judging you. And it brings together people from all over the world." He lived at 20 East 8th St. in a top-floor walk-up with a skylight in the 1960s.

When he studied for his Ph.D. in clinical psychology at Columbia in the '60s, "they required us to tell gays they were sick." It was his own experience with "a friend who confided that he was gay and had gone home with a sailor who threatened to kill him, escaping on a narrow ledge," that drew him into the issue and spurred his revolutionary thesis. "I would never consider a patient healthy unless he had overcome his prejudice against homosexuality," he wrote.

Weinberg continues to help people understand themselves through his therapy and writing, in 2003, *Why Men Won't Commit.* His own commitment to freeing people from their hang-ups is singular.

Edmund White

AUTHOR

"I first lived in the Village from 1962 to '68 on MacDougal Street between Bleecker and Houston," Edmund White, a Midwest native, said. "It was in a $100-a-month three-room walk-up in a tenement across the street from a beautiful building where Bob Dylan lived."

He would hang out at the Hip Bagel where he recalls that he "would eat and talk with this very fat woman who turned out to be Mama Cass. After that, anybody who told me they were going to be a big star, I believed."

He remembers his roommate dated the playwright Lanford Wilson, who in those days "was so poor, we'd feed him every night. He was determined to live by the pen."

The Village was "still cheap" in those days, as White put it, with "an awful lot of artists and old Italian couples who spoke Italian to each other—it was a nice mix." He said it was "also possible for someone to be a waiter three nights a week and support themselves. Now you'd have to be kept!"

White lived for 16 years in Paris and now is back in New York in Chelsea. He has given us such evocative novels as *Nocturnes for the King of Naples*, *A Boy's Own Story*," *The Beautiful Room is Empty*, *The Farewell Symphony*, and *The Married Man*. He co-authored the groundbreaking *Joy of Gay Sex* and chronicled *States of Desire: Travels in Gay America*. And the pleasures of just moving about in a historic city are captured in his *The Flâneur: A Stroll through the Paradoxes of Paris*.

With other writers who are gay, he formed the Violet Quill, many of the members of which have been lost to AIDS including Robert Ferro, Michael Grumley, Christopher Cox and George Whitmore. Edmund White is a survivor who has lived to tell the tale.

Margaret Whiting

SINGER AND ACTRESS

She had a hit with *That Old Black Magic* in 1942 and first recorded her signature song, *Moonlight in Vermont* in 1944. A member of the Songwriters' Hall of Fame, Margaret Whiting has twelve gold records. She had a TV series, *The Whiting Girls*, in 1955 with her sister, Barbara. When she toured with singers Rosemary Clooney, Kay Starr and Helen O'Connell as well as comediennes Rosemarie, Martha Raye and Kaye Ballard in an act called "4 Girls 4," their driver was future movie star George Clooney for a time. She has worked with all the greats–from Cole Porter and Hoagy Carmichael to Mel Torme and Bing Crosby.

Some of the songs with which Whiting is most identified include Rodgers' and Hammerstein's *It Might as Well Be Spring* (recorded with Dick Haymes), *Slipping Around* with country star Jimmy Wakely, *Now is the Hour*, *Far Away Places* and *Tenderly* by Walter Gross and Jack Lawrence. She has done Broadway shows such as *Gypsy*, *Pal Joey* and *Call Me Madam* as well as *Dream*, the salute to Johnny Mercer. On TV, she appeared with Bob Hope and as a regular on the Jack Smith Show. She is also famous for her life-long commitment to helping young talent develop and is chairperson of the Johnny Mercer Charitable Foundation.

Whiting often performs her cabaret act in the Village, and remembered working at Eighty Eights where "I saw some wonderful girls that were going to be stars like Nancy Lamont and Karen Mason." With her husband, Jack Wrangler, she did many benefits there on behalf of AIDS charities.

But she had a real Village experience at the Halloween Parade one year. "A woman dressed as nun came up to me and asked, 'How are you?' I said I was fine. 'It's nice to see you,' the nun said, 'but don't you recognize me?" Whiting gave her a blank look. "I'm your daughter," the "nun" said. It really was her daughter Debbie.

Randolfe "Randy" Wicker

CIVIL RIGHTS PIONEER

Long before the Stonewall Rebellion in New York in 1969, Randy Wicker was a prominent gay activist. After moving from Texas where he did civil rights work, he lived in the Village in the 1960s, recalling it as a "real community." In 1962, he was the first person to go on a radio show in which gay people spoke for themselves. In 1964, he was the first out gay person on TV and organized the first public gay demonstration, protesting the ban on gays in the military—a fight still being contested.

Here Wicker is pictured in Julius', a legendary gay bar on West 10th Street. But in 1965, he said, "I was one of five people who went into the bar demanding to be served, challenging the law that said you could not serve alcohol to homosexuals or allow us to gather." With Dick Leitsch, the president of the Mattachine Society, an early gay group, the late Craig Rodwell, who founded the Oscar Wilde Bookshop, and John Timmons, among others, "we had gone to some straight bars like Howard Johnson's to contest the law, announcing ourselves as gay and they served us. But Julius' was at that time worried about 'turning' gay and we were refused." Wicker and company went to court and the State Liquor Authority had to change the regulation.

From 1974 to 2003, he was the proprietor of Randy Wicker's Uplift Lighting, a lamp store on Hudson above Christopher. "The rent began at $150/month and ended at $5,600/month."

Today, Wicker is a nationally known spokesperson for the human cloning movement. "I'm not through living," he said. "I want my genotype to live on beyond me."

Doric Wilson

Playwright Doric Wilson didn't just survive the 1969 Stonewall Riots that birthed the modern gay movement, he has also survived working in New York's off-off Broadway theatre. His first play *And He Made Her* opened at the famed Caffe Cino (where his photo here was taken) in 1961, starring Jane Lowry and Paxton Whitehead. Legendary producer Richard Barr invited him to become a member of the Playwright's Unit and by the mid-1960s he helped found the Circle Repertory Theater.

Wilson grew up on his granddad's ranch in Washington State where he failed English because his teacher thought he must have plagiarized the play he wrote as an assignment…because it was so sophisticated.

After Stonewall, Wilson joined the early Gay Activists Alliance and supplemented his theatre work as a bartender and manager, opening such places as the Spike, Ty's, and Brothers and Sisters Cabaret. With partners Billy Blackwell, John McSpadden and Peter del Valle, he founded The Other Side of Silence (TOSOS), the first out gay professional theatre company doing work by Behan, Coward, Orton, Terrence McNally, Robert Patrick, Martin Sherman and Lanford Wilson, as well as his own. With Barry Childs and Mark Finley, they revived the group in 2001 and TOSOS II is going strong. Wilson's *Street Theater* dealt with the Stonewall Riots and *The West Street Gang* was about gay people who physically fought back against gay-bashing. He received the first Robert Chesley Award for Lifetime Achievement in Gay Theatre.

Edward Albee once told Wilson at the old New Colony Bar that he was "too nice to be a playwright," but Wilson's life in the theatre shows just how well nice guys can do. "The wonderful words, the laughter, the impossible made magic by the ringing of a bell—that's what I remember most," he wrote, referring to the Cino. "I remember everything but the dates."

Julie Wilson

SINGER AND ACTRESS

The Village was always there, but it took a while for veteran torch singer Julie Wilson to find it.

"When I came to New York as chorus girl, first at the Latin Quarter and then at the Copacabana, we did five shows a night, seven nights a week. If I went out, it was for breakfast at Reuben's around four or five in the morning. There was no time to enjoy all that Greenwich Village or New York had to offer.

"Later, after I became a solo performer, I would always get lost when I came to the Village. I always used the subways and when I would get off in the Village, the streets confused me. In 1969, I went to have dinner with the man who still does my makeup and got so lost that I was two hours late.

"In 1976, I retired to Omaha to raise my sons and care for my parents. It was only when I returned in 1986 that the Village began to play such an important role in my life. Going to the clubs and encouraging the young performers. Doing AIDS benefits at Eighty Eights or performing at the Gay Community Center. And where else can I go after a late performance to eat, walking down Bleecker Street still wearing my gown, gardenia, and eyelashes with my fuzzy schnauzer slippers on my lousy feet! And I have been known to look like a bag lady as I wait for the PATH train at the Christopher Street Station."

Nancy Wilson

SINGER

Nancy Wilson, the incomparable song stylist, recalled her first impression of Greenwich Village: "When I first moved to New York in the mid-late '50s to pursue my career, I went on an expedition of Manhattan, section by section.

"I had heard of the bohemian lifestyle of the Village, but it was the music, university, artists, bookstores, parks, cemeteries and the architecture that brought me there to explore. Of course, the night clubs of the Village were also of interest. The Bitter End for comedy. Village Gate for straight-ahead jazz and off-Broadway productions. Sheridan Square Playhouse to watch Colleen Dewhurst, Martin Sheen and many others hone their craft. Wanted to see where old Café Society was located, which closed before I arrived in New York. One Sheridan Square (home of Café Society, later theatres). Piano bars at 55 and 59 Grove St., Max Gordon's Village Vanguard, Julius', Nick's, Five Spot and the Blue Note. I did do a little studying there, just watching. Almost forgot Hollywood on the Hudson.

"The sights, sounds, smells of the Village have always had an international flavor to me and I can walk and spend many, many hours exploring—one of my favorite things to do."

Today, the Grammy (*How Glad I Am*) and Emmy (*The Nancy Wilson Show*) award-winning artist who has recorded more than sixty albums still makes room on her schedule for gigs at the Blue Note on West 3rd Street.

"Labels don't mean anything to me," Nancy Wilson said. "I sing songs."

Peter Yarrow

FOLK SINGER AND HUMAN RIGHTS ACTIVIST

Peter Yarrow started playing in the Village with Peter, Paul and Mary almost 40 years ago. Since then, he has picked up five Grammy Awards with the group and an Emmy nomination on his own.

"Greenwich Village in the early 1960's," he recalled, "was a place of enormous energy, a crucible of creative activity. The air was filled with excitement. Something remarkable was happening and everything was changing. Folksingers and poets started their days as the sun went down, converging on the myriad of coffee houses, the seats of the new truth, the new sensibility. It was not about money or power or the promise of fame. It was about discovery, hope, a new order, idealism, justice, equality, freedom. Guitar strings shimmered or voices pleaded and wept their universal longing for a better way, a better world. Believers all, it may have been our finest hour."

Lenore Zola

SAVED THE VILLAGE NURSING HOME

The Village has a lot of heart. When the Village Nursing Home on West 12th Street was threatened with closure in 1977, people like Lenore Zola stepped in.

"Neighbors saw old people being put out on the street with bags. At that time, the Caring Community, a local lunch program for the elderly, had $300 in the bank," she said, "and the budget for the Home was millions. We accepted the responsibility. To start, $275,000 had to be raised in a year and the whole community got involved. It even stayed open during the renovation. Residents included the real Auntie Mame. Our whole purpose was not to ship our older neighbors all over the city. Keep it in the Village, in the family. This community has a soul. And relatives of the residents tell us that the care is good."

Lenore Zola died on November 1, 1998, at age 91.

Harriet Sohmers Zwerling

WRITER, TEACHER, ARTISTS' MODEL, BOHEMIAN

Harriet Sohmers Zwerling, author of *Notes of a Nude Model & other pieces* (Spuyten Duyvill, 2003), is a true Village bohemian who has hung out with María Irene Fornés, Susan Sontag, Seymour Krim, Alfred Chester, and Norman Mailer and two of his wives.

Poet Edward Field, himself a Village legend, wrote, "Harriet Zwerling's writing is the best self-portrait of her," so here she tells her own story that she calls "Village Dream:"

"When I was a teenager on the Upper West Side I dreamed of Greenwich Village, realm of sex, art and freedom, locus of all glamour. My favorite adventure was to take the open-top double-decker bus on Riverside Drive all the way downtown to Washington Square, fantasizing, as I flew through the summer air at eye-level with the grand Fifth Avenue buildings, that I belonged to the world of luxury and liberty swirling by on the street below. On arrival in the Square, I would settle myself on the rim of the fountain, the navel of the world, as I saw it, and pretend to be a Villager in my unfashionable girls' jeans and peasant blouse.

"At seventeen, my claim to citizenship in the republic of bohemia was strengthened when I became a freshman at NYU's Washington Square College. Now, I had a legitimate connection to this magical world, one which I soon expanded, hanging out at bars like the San Remo and the Kettle of Fish. I met people I thought of as real artists, was followed around by old men, like the photographer Weegee, and the painter Kaldis, who invited me to pose for them. What a thrill it was, although I was still not brave enough to actually do it. Ironic, this, since twenty years later I actually earned my living as an artists' model.

"I spent the '50s in Paris. When I returned to New York, the Cedar Tavern scene was in full swing and I was part of it, writing, editing the 'Provincetown Review,' posing at art schools and privately for painters like Raphael Soyer, smoking pot, sleeping around. I actually met my husband at the Cedar. In 1963, we were living on Sullivan Street and I gave birth to my son, Milo, now Milo Z, the brilliant funk musician whose band regularly plays the Village clubs.

"In spite of my uptown origins, I have always seen myself as a downtown girl, and now, in my late 70s, still claim that title."

Eve Fowler

1998
Bella Abzug
Betty Comden and Adolph Green
Tony Dapolito
Barry Harris
Rose James
Ed Koch
Connie Kopelov and Phyllis Siegel
Bishop Paul Moore
Helen Peters
Lawrence Quirk
Frank Riessman
Lenore Zola

Bela Borsodi

1999
Amy Ashworth
Keith Crandell
Lewis Harrison
Luther Henderson
Kim Hunter
Lainie Kazan
Larry Kramer
Jimmy Lou
Dr. Erline Perkins McGriff
Rev. Howard Moody
Jack Newfield
Sister Marita Rose O'Brien
David Webster

Steve Hill

2000
Joan Bach
Mordecai and Irma Bauman
Ed Burnett
Merce Cunningham
Tommy Flanagan
Vivian Gornick
Uta Hagen
Jay Oliva
Dr. Joseph Sonnabend
Calvin Trillin
Julie Wilson

2001
Blanche Wiesen Cook
Germán Diez
Art D'Lugoff
Miriam Friedlander
Dennis Dugan
Diana Kan
Alfred Levitt
Sylvia Rivera
Florence Rush
Eileen Storey
Nancy Wilson
Peter Yarrow

2002
Edward Albee
Wayne Barrett
Susan Brownmiller
André De Shields
Edward Field and Neil Derrick
Kitty Carlisle Hart
Geoffrey Holder
Bettye Lane
Ralph Lee
Sylvia Miles
Ellen Stewart
Margaret Whiting

Craig Wallace Dale

2003
Anthony Amato
Ramsey Clark
Crystal Field
Frances Goldin
Anne Jackson and Eli Wallach
Al Lewis
Robin Morgan
Joan Nestle
Odetta
Ned Rorem
Susan Sarandon
William Wynkoop and Roy Strickland

2004
Jimmy Breslin and Ronnie Eldridge
Charlotte Carter
Mel Gussow
Celeste Holm
Arthur Laurents
Fred W. McDarrah
Philip Pavia
Rev. Herb Rogers, SJ
Frances Sternhagen
Catharine Stimpson
Edmund White
Doric Wilson

2005
Ann Bannon
Patti Bown
Paul Colby
Judy Collins
Jules Feiffer
Barbara Garson
Lesley Gore
Darlene Love
David Margulies
Malachy McCourt
Bruce Morrow – Cousin Brucie
Randolph "Randy" Wicker

2006
Jane Alexander
Rev. Daniel Berrigan
Karl Bissinger
E. L. Doctorow
Joyce Gold
Margo Jefferson
Frank McCourt
David McReynolds
Estelle Parson
Rollerena
John & Mark Sebastian
Marian Seldes

2007
Kaye Ballard
Norma Becker
Kathleen Chalfant
Chuck Close
Samuel Delany
Carol Greitzer
Richard Howard
Stanley Kunitz
Lynn Redgrave
Jerry Tallmer
George Weinberg
Harriet Sohmers Zwerling